Cryptids

and Other Creepy Creatures

Cryptids
and Other Creepy Creatures

JOHN D. WRIGHT

tangerine Press

an imprint of
SCHOLASTIC
www.scholastic.com

an imprint of
SCHOLASTIC
www.scholastic.com

Scholastic and Tangerine Press and associated logos are trademarks
and/or registered trademarks of Scholastic Inc.

Published by Tangerine Press, an imprint of Scholastic Inc.,
557 Broadway; New York, NY 10012

Scholastic Canada Ltd.
Markham, Ontario

Scholastic Australia Pty. Ltd
Gosford NSW

Scholastic New Zealand Ltd.
Greenmount, Auckland

Grolier International Inc
Makati City, Philippines

10 9 8 7 6 5 4 3 2 1

ISBN-10: 0-545-11959-6
ISBN-13: 978-0-545-11959-7

Editorial and design by
Amber Books Ltd
Bradley's Close
74–77 White Lion Street
London N1 9PF
United Kingdom
www.amberbooks.co.uk

Project Editor: Sarah Uttridge
Design: Andrew Easton
Illustrations: Mike Moran

Printed in Singapore

Picture credits:
All illustrations by Mike Moran © Amber Books Ltd.

Contents

Introduction

Cryptids are creatures that some people believe are real, although scientists have not been able to prove they exist. The term is too new to appear in most dictionaries, but people are familiar with many examples, such as the Loch Ness Monster and Bigfoot. These "monsters" exist somewhere between fantasy and science. The continuous sightings of them sound real enough and could be true or partly true.

In many cases, investigators are still searching for definitive proof. This is why professional teams keep probing the depths of Loch Ness for its shy serpent, and British scientists in 2008 conducted DNA tests on hairs found in India that some believe are from Yeti.

Here we have selected a variety of amazing stories passed down orally through generations, like the dinosaurlike creatures in deepest Africa. Included in the ghoulish bunch is the Chupacabra in Puerto Rico, which kills animals and drains their bodies of blood. Some monsters like Bigfoot actually run frightened from us.

Another group of stories involves ghosts. Many have long existed, including the spirit that haunts Glamis Castle in Scotland, and America has its share, like the ghost prisoners of Alcatraz.

Among the strange creatures in our collection are a group known as urban myths or urban legends. These include stories of normal animals in spooky situations, such as alligators crawling through the sewers of New York and Mexican pets that turn out to be repulsive creatures after they settle into family homes.

We have also added several weird phenomena that cannot be explained, such as spontaneous human combustion and the Bermuda Triangle. You can decide which of these beasts and events sound real. After all, thousands of people say they have seen ghosts or UFOs. The truth may lie beyond science, but the search is always fascinating

Loch Ness Monster

The most famous water monster is a giant serpent living in a loch (lake) in the Highlands of Scotland. This is a perfect hiding place, because Loch Ness is 24 miles (38 km) long and 755 feet (230 m) deep and very dark. Despite this, thousands of people have reported sightings of a monster with a long neck and humped back. It is so familiar, locals have nicknamed it "Nessie." Scientific teams, including several from the United States, have searched for this elusive underwater creature using everything from sonar to infrared photography. They have occasionally located unknown shapes and strange animal echoes or calls. However, skeptics say Nessie is a myth, and their case was helped when the best-known photo of the beast was revealed to be a hoax. Some believe the "monster" is a large eel or fish like a sturgeon, but others say it could be a prehistoric whale or unknown species.

▶ Nessie has not only attracted tourists. Kevin Carlyon, high priest of the British Coven of White Witches, has also been a visitor to the loch. In 2001, he cast a spell to protect Nessie from a Swedish science group that intended to trap the monster. Sightings became few, and two years later Carlyon returned on Friday the 13th to undo the spell slightly. For this, he made a circle of stones and burned incense while casting a new spell. He said Nessie would still be protected, "but she will be able to come back again and thrill the public." In fact, more sightings were soon reported.

Where in the World?

Loch Ness is in northwestern Scotland, forming part of the Caledonian Canal that runs across the Highlands from the North Sea to the Atlantic Ocean. The Ness River connects the loch to the North Sea.

● LOCH NESS, SCOTLAND

Did You Know?

● Robert Rines, a Boston lawyer and inventor, has searched for Nessie for 37 years. His underwater photography once captured an image of an animal's body, neck, head, and flipper. In 2008, however, 85-year-old Rines made his last expedition to the loch, saying "Unfortunately, I'm running out of age."

● Several boats, including research vessels, offer cruises on Loch Ness throughout the year. Tourists are able to search the hidden depths using sonar and video equipment. One boat is even named "Nessie Hunter." Along the way are impressive views of the ancient ruins of Urquhart Castle, which overlooks the loch.

● People even use the Internet to try spotting Nessie. One Scottish site includes what is claimed to be a recording of Nessie's sounds, previous pictures of the creature, and the official Loch Ness Monster Fan Club, which lists recent sightings.

Thetis Lake Monster

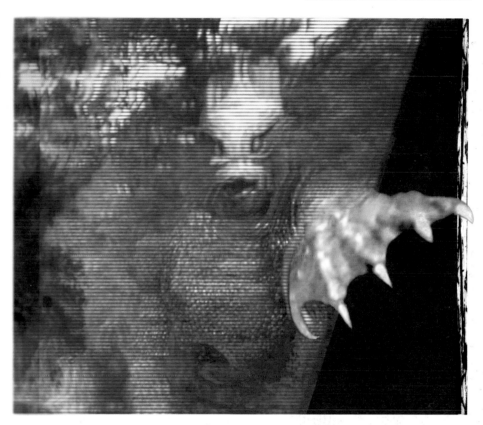

Although it only appeared twice in 1972, the aggressive scaly monster of Thetis Lake in Canada's Vancouver Island struck fear into the two teenage boys who encountered it and provoked an investigation by the Royal Canadian Mounted Police. The creature chased the youths, and one claimed a cut on his hand was caused by its spiky fin. They said the monster was 5 feet (1.5 m) tall and resembled a human lizard with a horrible head and barbed spikes protruding from its skull. Four days later, two men saw it surface in the lake, glance around, and submerge again. They gave a similar description, saying its body was covered with silvery scales. Within the week, a man reported the disappearance in the previous year of his pet Tegu lizard, which is an aggressive animal that can grow to 4 feet (1.2 m). The Mounties closed their investigation, but many locals disagreed with this easy answer.

▶ Few creatures have such dreadful features as the Thetis Lake Monster, with its dark and bulbous eyes, fishlike face, and horrifying webbed claws. Some have said this strange animal might be caught in an evolutionary trap halfway between a fish and a primate. Because the monster has not surfaced in recent years, people using the lake for recreational purposes have little fear of an attack. Many of the swimmers, canoers, and kayakers are not aware that a creature supposedly lurks beneath the waters. However, one guidebook, published in 1998, advised people to carry a flaming torch to deter the lake monster.

Where in the World?

The lake's park is about a 20-minute drive on the Trans-Canada Highway from the city of Victoria. This is the southern tip of Vancouver Island, the largest island on the west coast of the Americas.

● VANCOUVER ISLAND

Did You Know?

● The sightings of the Thetis Lake Monster happened in the Pacific Northwest, where Native American people once believed monstrous creatures lived in their misty lakes and rivers. The Kwakiutl people of Vancouver Island, for instance, feared Pugwis, a fierce undersea monster with a human form but a fishlike face and gills.

● The Thetis Lake Monster is eerily similar to the monster created by Hollywood for the popular 1954 movie *The Creature from the Black Lagoon* and its two sequels. That half-man, half-fish beast from the Amazon River had the same scales and overall look, made more scary by being filmed in 3D.

● Thetis Lake is popular for swimming and boating, and is also surrounded by scenic trails. Named Canada's first official nature sanctuary in 1958, the area became Thetis Lake Regional Park in 1993 and now receives 150,000 visitors each year. It is undergoing a restoration project to be completed in 2009.

Morgawr

If the Loch Ness Monster has a relative, it surely is Morgawr, which has the same long neck and humped back. Morgawr, however, is a sea serpent in Falmouth Bay off the British coast of Cornwall, while Nessie dwells in a freshwater lake in Scotland. In the old Cornish language, Morgawr means "Sea Giant." Various monster-spotters described Morgawr as black or dark brown with a snakelike head, stumpy horns, a large hump-backed body, scaly legs, and flippers. One eyewitness estimated its length to be 40 feet (12 m). Local people first feared these creatures in 1876, when fishermen caught a "monster" with a long neck. In 1976 photographs of Morgawr were published in the Falmouth newspaper and shown on BBC television; then in 1999 a video was made. Though some doubt Morgawr is a monster, others say it could be a plesiosaur, believed to be extinct for more than 65 million years.

▶ The fearsome cliffs and ruins along the Cornish coast provide a moody setting for anyone hunting Morgawr. The black curl of the monster's back has shocked scores of hearty walkers exploring the area. Locals advise those who are seriously interested in seeing the creature to station themselves at one of the less accessible parts of "Morgawr's Mile." Although the shy monster rarely comes to the surface, the long wait can be worth the trouble. A well-known writer, Sheila Bird, spotted Morgawr from the cliffs in July 1985 on a clear evening and described it as "a most beautiful, magnificent creature."

Where in the World?

Falmouth Bay is part of the English Channel along the Cornish peninsula. The coastline adjacent to the mouth of the Helford River has been nicknamed "Morgawr's Mile" because of the many sightings of the monster in the area.

● ENGLISH CHANNEL

Did You Know?

● Michael McCormick, a showman from Alburquerque, New Mexico, who called himself a "professor of metaphysics," arrived in Cornwall in the spring of 1976 with the intention of capturing Morgawr. He hoped to add the monster to his traveling exhibition, but after a month of searching he left Cornwall without sighting his elusive prey.

● Morgawr has also been called a supernatural being. Tony "Doc" Shiels, a psychic and professional "Wizard of the Western World," said the monster may be a "parapsychical entity" that has more than three dimensions. He suggested that Morgawr can change its shape and size, even assuming a totally different look.

● Other strange events have been recorded around Falmouth Bay. In the 1970s, UFOs were reported and photographs taken of "piskies" (who are supposed to be Cornish fairies) with red hair and wrinkled faces. Also, a tourist once spied a "huge great thing with feathers, like a big man with flapping wings."

Lake Tianchi Monster

For more than a century, the Chinese have recorded a school of monsters living in Lake Tianchi, which at 7,180 feet (2,189 m) is the world's highest volcanic lake. Local government officials in July 2003 saw as many as 20 of the mysterious creatures swimming together for nearly an hour. That same month, a group of soldiers watched a monster swimming for a few minutes and described it as blackish-green with scales on its back and a round head with horns. Another sighting, however, said the animal had smooth, gray skin, a humanlike head with a protruding mouth, big round eyes, and a neck that measured up to 5 feet (1.5 m) with a white ring mark at its base. The best documentation was made in 2007 by the director of a local TV station, who shot a 20-minute video of six black Lake Tianchi monsters who had been "swimming and frolicking" for an hour and a half.

▶ The lake rests on top of towering Mount Changbai, which is a famous scenic spot that attracts tourists from around the world, as well as leaders from China and other nations. Even more visits are expected now that the *Guinness Book of World Records* is adding entries for the high lake and nearby waterfall. The calm beauty of Lake Tianchi can be very deceptive, however, because of the many monster sightings that have been reported since the beginning of the twentieth century. Some scientists dispute this, saying the lake is much too cold for a large creature to survive there.

Where in the World?

Lake Tianchi forms a border between China and North Korea. Stretching 3 miles (4.84 km) north–south and 2 miles (3.35 km) east–west, the cold lake extends from Jilin Province in China into Ryanggang Province in North Korea.

● LAKE TIANCHI

Did You Know?

● Another type of monster appeared in 1903, with eyewitnesses saying it resembled a huge buffalo. The animal gave a roar and leapt from the water in an effort to attack three people, but one of them shot it six times. The beast roared again and dived back into the lake.

● Zhuo Yongsheng, who recorded the unknown creatures, was amazed at their swimming abilities. "They could swim as fast as yachts," he said, "and at times they would disappear under the water. It was impressive to see them all swimming at exactly the same pace, as if someone was giving orders."

● Lake Tianchi means "Pearl of Heavenly Mountain." Its water comes from melted snow on the Silent Mountains. It is China's deepest mountain lake, and has an average depth of 669 feet (204 m). It flows to the nearby Changbai Waterfall, which drops 223 feet (68 m). This is the world's largest waterfall that is fed by a crater lake.

Mokele-mbembe

Do dinosaurs still exist in a remote part of the world? Some natives in the African country of the Congo Republic are certain they have seen a gigantic creature that resembles a sauropod, believed extinct for some 65 million years. Its three-claw tracks were first seen in 1776, and sightings of the animal in the jungle swamps have been going on for more than a century. Locals have named the beast Mokele-mbembe, which means "one who stops the flow of rivers." Its size is said to be between that of a hippopotamus and that of an elephant. Eyewitnesses agree that it has a smooth grayish-brown skin, a long neck, a long tail like a crocodile's, and a small head topped with a horn or frill like a rooster. They say it only eats plants but will quickly kill those who approach too near. Pygmies in the Congo add that Mokele-mbembe sleeps on a bed of elephants' tusks.

▶ Pygmies have long recounted tales of terrifying battles with the Mokele-mbembe, but the only solid evidence of its existence are the large footprints that have been recorded for more than 200 years. Some of the most impressive ones were found in 1932 in central Africa by an expedition to find Mokele-mbembe led by Ivan T. Sanderson, a noted American cryptozoologist (someone who studies animals whose existence is disputed). The prints were as large as hippopotamus tracks, but that animal was unknown in the region. Natives say that hippos are never found where Mokele-mbembe lives, because the monster kills them.

Where in the World?

The Congo Republic is in central Africa and is sometimes confused with its eastern neighbor, the larger Congo. Mokele-mbembe sightings have been around Lake Tele and the swamps and rivers in the northern Likouala jungle region.

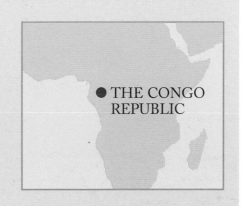

● THE CONGO REPUBLIC

Did You Know?

● Around 1960, pygmy fishermen built a stake barrier to keep the Mokele-mbembe out of Lake Tele. They claim they killed one with spears when it tried to break through. Their people took days to cut up the large beast for a victory feast, but all who ate its meat soon died.

● In 1920, the Smithsonian Institution in Washington, D.C., sent out an expedition of 32 men to find Mokele-mbembe. They discovered unknown tracks and heard strange roars from a swamp. The expedition ended tragically when four members were killed in a train derailment in an area where a tribe said they had seen the monster.

● Sauropod means "lizard-hipped." They lived about 100 million years, longer than most dinosaurs. A familiar member of the family is Apatosaurus (formerly named Brontosaurus). Sauropods have been found on all continents except Antarctica. They existed during the Jurassic Period (206–144 million years ago) in North America, where four or five various types coexisted.

Ogopogo

Canada's most famous lake monster was known to the First Nations people as N'ha-a-itk, or "lake demon." The animal was said to live in British Columbia's Lake Okanagan, which reaches a depth of nearly 1,000 feet (305 m). The monster supposedly hides in an underwater cave near Rattlesnake Island. Native Peoples paddling canoes near the spot would toss live offerings, such as a chicken, into the waters to please it. White settlers also saw the monster and by 1924 a song renamed it Ogopogo. Most described it as having a dark snakelike body about 82 feet (25 m) long with several humps, and a large head resembling a horse or goat. Several films have been made from a distance, and sightings continue at the rate of about six a year. Many believe Ogopogo is a normal animal, but one zoologist suggested it was a primitive whale, Basilosaurus, which flourished 40 million years ago.

▶ The territorial waters of Ogopogo are found in the irregular outline of Lake Okanagan. Located in the high latitudes of North America, the lake hides the monster's underwater lair near Rattlesnake Island. When a new ferry was built in 1926 to cross the surface, the government announced that it would be equipped with several devices designed to repel monsters. Some locals were worried about Ogopogo ramming the lake's floating bridge, but maintenance crews have not reported any serious damage. Ogopogo's fame has drawn international media to the lake, with television documentaries being broadcast worldwide.

Where in the World?

Lake Okanagan lies in the scenic south-central region of British Columbia, Canada's most western province. Ogopogo's cave is said to be at Squally Point, a stretch of water near Rattlesnake Island, facing the town of Peachland.

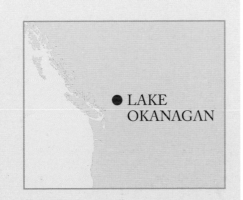

● LAKE OKANAGAN

Did You Know?

● John McDougal, an early settler in the area, had an eerie encounter in 1860 with something below Lake Okanagan. He was swimming two horses across behind his canoe, and they were pulled beneath the waves. He managed to save himself by cutting the ropes to the horses, which were never seen again.

● The Grey Monk Estate Winery, which has vineyards right down to Lake Okanagan, was designated an official "Ogopogo Viewing Station" and has offered a $2 million prize to anyone who can prove conclusively that the monster exists. The winery even receives calls from children asking for details about Ogopogo's habits.

● The city of Kelowna has a statue of Ogopogo in a park next to the lake. It resembles the Loch Ness Monster, showing a head, two humps, and a tail rising above ground. Kelowna is midway on the 80-mile (129-km) lake, and Ogopogo is said to live 12.5 miles (20 km) away.

Cadborosaurus willsi

I t bears an impressive Latin name, but this giant sea serpent is just known as "Caddy" to people along Canada's Pacific coast. The Manhousat First Nation called it Hiyitl'iik, meaning "he who moves by wriggling side to side." Two marine scientists made the new name official because the creature is mostly spotted in Cadboro Bay. A dead juvenile specimen was said to be taken from the stomach of a sperm whale in 1937. Photos were made but the specimen was mysteriously lost on the way to testing. Many observers have said Caddy is up to 49 feet (15 m) in length and has a head like a horse or camel, vertical body humps, two pairs of flippers, and a spiky tail. Its speed on the surface has been measured at up to 40 knots (46 miles per hour/74 kph). People on shore still frequently see Caddy, a species unknown to scientists.

▶ This native image, which fits the description of Caddy, has been traditionally used throughout Alaska. It indicates that the creature moves north when Vancouver waters begin to warm. One researcher counted 101 sightings during Vancouver's cold periods and only 64 in warm times. The Inuit of Alaska have even painted the image on their canoes to ward off attacks by the beast. Caddy is known to travel as far north as the Bering Strait. In that sea passage between Alaska and Siberia, the people in Nunivak Island call it Pal Rai Yuk, while those on Kin Island name it Tizheruk.

Where in the World?

Cadborosaurus willsi lives off southern Victoria Island in the Canadian province of British Columbia. This same island is home to the Thetis Lake Monster, although Caddy's larger realm is in the sea at Cadboro Bay.

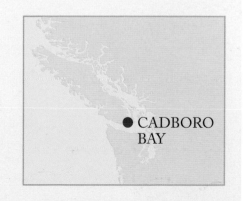

● CADBORO BAY

Did You Know?

● A slightly smaller Cadborosaurus willsi has also been observed. Locals call it Amy, believing the animal to be Caddy's mate. In 1968 a baby that might have been Caddy and Amy's offspring was captured by a fisherman. The infant measured only 16 inches (40.6 cm), but it already had sharp teeth and flippers just developing.

● A longtime Caddy hunter, Ernest Lee, said he had accidentally rammed it twice with his motorboat in 1943. The creature became still and sank into the deep water, apparently dead. Locals became angry over the tragedy, but Lee's reputation was saved when Caddy resurfaced in good health two weeks later.

● If someone sees Caddy, the Oak Bay Tourism office advises, "A slow approach is recommended during a close encounter with Caddy. Maintain a comfortable distance and always leave an escape route. Never come closer than 100 feet (30.5 m) of a small animal, because a nearby parent may intervene to protect its offspring."

Yeti

Natives in the towering Himalayan Mountains of Asia have long feared Yeti, a fierce apelike creature. He is also known as the Abominable Snowman, because the giant monster roams his lonely realm of snow and ice, leaving massive footprints as evidence of his existence. The Sherpa people of Nepal and Tibet have heard his howls and tell horrible stories of the beast's attacks on humans and animals, and of villagers being carried off by Yeti. Observers agree that Yeti is huge and covered with thick reddish-brown fur, but in the higher regions he is more pale for camouflage. Several scientific teams have searched for the monster. They have seen unknown creatures in the distance, photographed many large footprints, and viewed fur specimens that locals said were from the Yeti. Analyses of some of the fur samples were unknown to science and could not be identified.

▶ The peaks of the Himalayas make a bleak home and hiding place for Yeti. In this frozen world, footprints can remain throughout the year. Mountain climbers like Edmund Hillary have spotted the prints while scaling Mount Everest. The first photographs of the prints were taken on Everest in 1951 by Eric Shipton and Michael Ward at nearly 20,000 feet (6,100 m). The prints were clearly made by a two-legged being. An American expedition in 2007 measured footprints 13 inches (33 cm) long with five toes 10 inches (25 cm) wide. Doubters claim that ordinary animals leave such tracks that expand when the snow partially melts.

Where in the World?

Asia's Himalayas are the highest mountain range in the world. The Yeti has been sighted mostly in the region of Tibet, which is part of China, and its southern neighbors, the countries of Nepal and Bhutan.

● HIMALAYAS

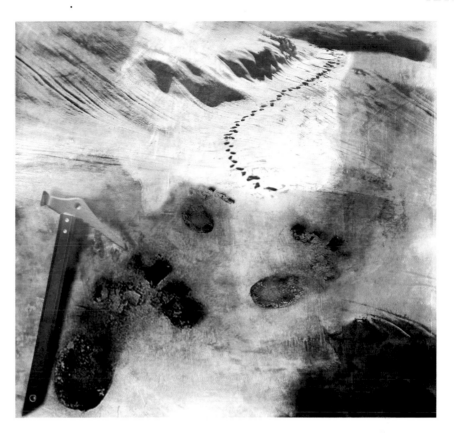

Did You Know?

● In 2008, the British artist Polyanna Pickering made a photo-fit of Yeti from descriptions by people who had seen him in the country of Bhutan. She sketched as the eyewitnesses clustered around her and suggested refinements to the image. Pickering also sketched a supposed yeti scalp kept in a monastery.

● A vivid Yeti encounter was reported in 1938 by a Captain d'Auvergue of Calcutta, India. He had been blinded by a snowstorm while he was alone in the Himalayas. As he neared death from hypothermia, a 9-foot (2.7-m) Yeti appeared and sheltered him from the blizzard. When d'Auvergue recovered, the creature had disappeared.

● Mysterious creatures in other countries have been given the name Yeti. Sumatra has a "jungle yeti" that seems to be an unknown species of ape that walks like a man. In Siberia in 2003 a furry Yeti was discovered in the permafrost, but tests showed the bones were several thousand years old.

Skunk Ape

One monster story is a real stinker. The Bigfoot type of animal living in Florida's Everglades has earned his name of "skunk ape" because he smells like a mixture of rotten eggs, moldy cheese, and hydrogen sulfide. Locals say his foul odor comes from living in empty alligator caves in the swamp where decaying matter produces methane gas. Otherwise, the reclusive creature has never attacked people, though some say he may be responsible for people disappearing in the Everglades. Sightings have been made for at least a century—there were many in the 1970s and several more recently. A giant skunk ape shocked two European women in 2003 while they photographed plants, but they escaped. A year later, a woman driving home at sunset on a rural road encountered a long-haired creature who rose up to 8 feet (2.4 m). "When he saw me," she recalled, "he was as surprised as I was."

▶ Warnings about the skunk ape are frequently posted around the Everglades. Reminders are hardly needed by locals who have heard dreadful howls in the night and discovered strange footprints. Recent sightings continue, with one man in 2005 claiming the creature hit him over the head with a stick. These reports encouraged an expedition in 2008 by a 30-strong team from The Bigfoot Field Researchers Organization using video cameras, thermal imaging equipment, and microphones. But the skunk ape remains evasive when others invade his territory. He is said to have excellent hearing and will swim and climb trees to avoid humans.

Where in the World?

Most reports of skunk ape sightings occur in the swampy Everglades, a wilderness covering about 5,000 square miles (12,950 sq km) in southwestern Florida. Some of the encounters happen in other swamps around the state.

FLORIDA ●

Did You Know?

● In 2000, an anonymous Florida woman mailed two photos of a large apelike animal to her local sheriff's office. The creature had rummaged through her backyard in the countryside for three nights to steal apples, but disappeared before the police arrived. Many believe these are images of the skunk ape.

● The Skunk Ape Research Headquarters are located on a campsite in Ochopee, Florida. Brothers Dave and Jack Shealy operate the roadside building, collecting details of sightings and selling souvenirs that include skunk ape T-shirts and bumper stickers. An annual festival is held with a Miss Skunk Ape contest.

● The skunk ape has been used for two comedy horror movies. *Skunk Ape!?* (2003) featured punk rock music and even had the monster hanging onto the back of a minivan. *Stomp! Shout! Scream!* (2005) involved an all-girl garage rock band being stranded in a beach town and being terrorized by the creature.

Nguoi Rung

Sightings of Vietnam's wildman have been common, and even American soldiers during the war reported encounters with apelike creatures that resembled Bigfoot. The local name, Nguoi Rung, means "Forest People." Observers say the creature can be as small as 5 feet (1.5 m) or much larger, with fur ranging from gray to black. His footprints are larger than an ape's and wider than a human's and with much longer toes. This may be an unknown species, because the thick jungles hold many secrets. In recent years, zoologists have discovered several previously unknown mammals. Nguoi Rung could be one of these, such as an early apelike human. Some villagers believe he is an ordinary man who decades ago decided to return to the wild until his face and body were covered with fur. The creature is shy but reports say he will approach campfires and sit near people without speaking.

▶ The primitive face of Nguoi Rung has often shocked Vietnamese people going about their daily lives. Investigators say the beast normally eats fruit, leaves, insects, and mollusks, but sometimes small animals. Villagers who believe Nguoi Rung is a wildman say he has tattoos, makes frightening faces by widening his eyes, and has even been seen carrying a sword. In 1982 near the Cambodian border, Professor Tran Hong Viet of the Vietnam National University discovered a suspected footprint that measured 11 inches (28 cm) long and 6.3 inches (16 cm) wide. He made a cast that the country's scientists continue to study.

Where in the World?

Most reports of Nguoi Rung are centered in the Sa Thay district of Kontum province of Vietnam. This is known as the "three borders" region because the borders of Vietnam, Cambodia, and Laos meet here.

● VIETNAM

Did You Know?

● So many sightings of Nguoi Rung were reported during the Vietnam war that a communist general in 1974 sent a scientific team from Hanoi to locate the wildman. The searchers failed to find one but did bring back a cast of the creature's footprint (and, while they were at it, captured two elephants for the circus).

● In 2007 over the Cambodian border, a speechless jungle woman was captured, but her Nguoi Rung man escaped. A family identified her as their daughter who had disappeared 18 years before. They have tried to civilize her, but she has twice vanished into the jungle and returned, apparently hunting her mate.

● Among the new species discovered in Vietnam are a fast "skipper" butterfly, a white-lipped keelback snake, a new type of pheasant, a deer that is about the size of a large dog, and an animal that a naturalist said is "a kind of a goat, but a little bit strange."

Hibagon

The Japanese have a long history of mythical creatures, and Hibagon is the one most like Bigfoot and Yeti. Although its footprints are very large, about 10 inches (25 cm) long and 6 inches (15 cm) wide, the animal is smaller and looks like a combination of a man and a gorilla. Eyewitnesses say it is 5 feet (1.5 m) tall with thick black or brown fur, a face covered with bristles, a snubby nose, and fiercesome but intelligent eyes. An especially unpleasant aspect is its foul body smell. Sightings were first reported in 1970 when the creature was spotted in a rice paddy, and a photo was taken in 1974 as it hid behind a tree. Only two later encounters occurred, in 1980 and 1982, before Hibagon retreated into its forest around Mount Hiba in the prefecture (district) of Hiroshima. Hibagon would probably be insulted that its name was chosen by an animal control board.

▶ The awe-inspiring Mount Hiba overlooks Hibagon's realm in the lush forests below. The creature seems to have once lived on Hiba until an increase of game hunters eventually frightened it down. Some eyewitnesses say it has spots of white fur either on its chest, hands, arms, or feet. The monster is well-known in Japan, having been featured in books, magazines, and a 2005 movie, *Dear Hinagon*, using his less common name. Although many Japanese think Hibagon and Kappa (see Did You Know?) are the same, some locals have said Kappa resembles a monkey or human child rather than having the gorilla look of Hibagon.

Where in the World?

Hibagon lived around Mount Hiba in Hiroshima prefecture in southwestern Japan on the Seto Inland Sea. Its capital, Hiroshima, is the largest city. The prefecture is on Honshu Island, home to the famous Mount Fuji.

HIROSHIMA ●

Did You Know?

• People in the Mount Hiba region are proud to be associated with Hibagon. A statue of the creature stands alongside the road on the outskirts of Shobara City. Several cities sell souvenirs of Hibagon and manufacture monster-inspired sweets, including Hibagon eggs. Saijo City in Ehime prefecture adopted the animal as its symbol.

• Hibagon is sometimes called Kappa. The Japanese have encountered Kappa for centuries and disagree on whether the two creatures are the same species. Kappa are small and similar to apes, like Hibagon, but they usually live near, or even in, rivers. They seem more aggressive, sometimes attacking humans and sucking their blood.

• Mount Hiba, in the Hiroshima Citizen's Forest, has a great mythical history. An ancient chronicle said a goddess, Izanami no mokoto, was buried here after she lost her life giving birth to a fire god. Today she is honored on the mountain by an imperial mausoleum surrounded by beech trees.

Bigfoot

The frightening Bigfoot is probably the world's best-documented apelike creature, with sightings that stretch back more than 150 years. Bigfoot roams throughout the Pacific Northwest, and it is also known as Sasquatch in a First Nation language of Canada. More than 400 sightings have been reported of this beast, covered in thick shaggy brown hair and standing more than 6 feet 6 inches (2 m) tall with long arms dangling down to its knees. Although Bigfoot is known to be shy and rarely aggressive, he has tremendous strength and supposedly killed at least one hunter and a farmer's horse, which was found hanging high in a tree. In 1924, five miners reported that a band of the animals threw large rocks at their cabin. Although skeptics say the creature is a hoax or possibly just a bear, many researchers find it hard to discredit the best photos of Bigfoot and his giant footprints.

▶ A normal footprint is dwarfed by the famous imprint that gave Bigfoot its name. This happened in 1958 when construction workers in California discovered oversized footprints, and photos of the tracks in newspapers inspired the name. Reports of large apelike creatures in that region go back to the 1860s. However, after the death of one of the workers, his family said he had faked the footprints. Enormous tracks continue to be found. In 2006, a Canadian woman driving to Prince Albert, in Saskatchewan, spotted the creature near the highway, and men investigating that area found large footprints in the snow.

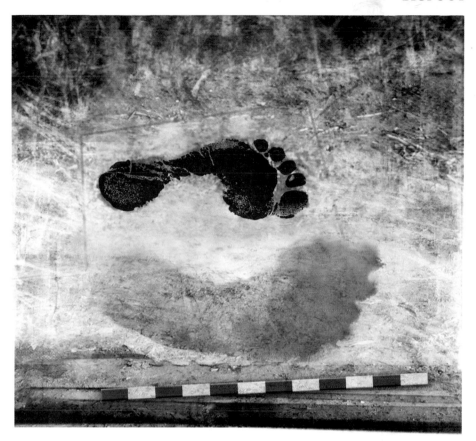

Where in the World?

Bigfoot has been sighted throughout the United States and Canada. Most encounters have been in the Pacific Northwest in the states of California, Oregon, and Washington and also in the Canadian province of British Columbia.

● CALIFORNIA

Did You Know?

● Before he was president, Theodore Roosevelt wrote about an encounter with Bigfoot told to him by a hunter named Bauman. He and another hunter had their camp destroyed by a beast who left large footprints. Bauman later found his companion dead with teeth marks in his throat and surrounded by the footprints.

● An awesome color movie of Bigfoot was made in 1967 by two men searching for it in northern California. They filmed the sudden appearance of a hairy creature walking away into the woods. Some think this was a man dressed as Bigfoot, but both observers believed the sighting was real.

● Bigfoot is said to be related to other giant human-apes found around the world. The comparison is often made with Yeti in the Himalayan Mountains, Hibagon in Japan, Nguoi Rung in Vietnam, and Yowie in Australia. Many other cultures have recorded such humanlike giants throughout history.

Fear Liath Mor

Scottish mountain climbers who have met Fear Liath Mor (Big Gray Man) say he could be supernatural. Sightings have been reported for hundreds of years on the summit and passes of Scotland's second-highest peak, Ben MacDhui, which rises 4296 feet (1309 m). Those climbers had entered the mist-filled territory of the giant ghost or animal described as being 10 feet (3 m) tall, covered in gray or brown hair with broad shoulders and long waving arms. His photographed footprints are 19 inches (49 cm) long and almost as wide, making them larger than those of Bigfoot. People who have encountered Fear Liath Mor reported a deadly coldness against their skin. Several felt fear and panic. In 1943 a mountaineer even fired three shots at the charging creature before fleeing.

▶ Magnificent Scottish thistles abound on the Cairngorm mountains, the beautiful but rough home of Fear Liath Mor. The many international climbers are unaware that locals have been terrified through the years by encounters with the monster along the lonely paths that slope down from Ben MacDhui, one of the six great peaks. The Gray Man's presence has been felt in many different ways, with hikers seeing the sky obscured by great dark blurs and hearing a high-pitched humming or singing. The famed climber John Norman Collie summed up his eerie encounter, saying. "I will not go back there myself, I know."

Where in the World?

Ben MacDhui is the highest peak in the Cairngorms, a mountain range in northeast central Scotland in the Grampian region. The mountains are east of the city of Aberdeen, which lies on the North Sea.

● CAIRNGORMS

Did You Know?

● Doubters think Fear Liath Mor may be a type of optical illusion that can occur in misty conditions. A well-known illusion is the specter of the brocken, which becomes visible when the sun is at a certain angle and is casting a person's shadow onto mist or low clouds. This creates an image of a large shadowy figure.

● The presence of the creature was reported in 1925 by John Norman Collie, a reputable mountain climber. He had heard an eerie crunch of footsteps behind his own during an ascent up the misty summit 35 years before. "I was seized with terror and took to my heels," he admitted.

● The bad conditions on Ben MacDhui have led to different descriptions of Fear Liath Mor. Witnesses have reported that he stands 20 feet (6 m) tall with a very straight posture and has an olive complexion, pointed ears, sharp talons on his toes, and was even reportedly wearing a top hat.

Mothman

Large glowing red eyes that seemed to hypnotize you. A flying speed of more than 100 miles an hour (160 kph). A high-pitched cry like a woman screaming. Indeed, this was a unique beast named Mothman by the terrified citizens of Point Pleasant, West Virginia. For 13 months from November 1966, the giant creature with large mothlike wings swooped down more than 100 times to observe and follow people. They said he was about 7 feet (5 m) tall with a wingspan of some 9 feet 10 inches (3 m). His gray skin seemed wrinkled to some. Mothman attacked no one, but his mission seemed linked to disaster. People reported their cars suddenly going dead and home electrical equipment failing. On the night of December 15, 1967, Point Pleasant's 700-foot (214-m) bridge over the Ohio River collapsed during rush hour, killing 46 people. After, Mothman was never seen again.

▶ Citizens of Point Pleasant found that you can't run from the Mothman. The first sighting was on a chilly fall night by two married couples driving 7 miles (11 km) north of the city. Spotting two red lights, they stopped the car and were terrified to see the glow was coming from the eyes of an enormous animal with wings. Accelerating away at more than 100 miles per hour (160 kph), the four eyewitnesses were stunned to see the bizarre creature fly into the air and stay over their Chevrolet at that high speed. When they reached the city limits, the Mothman turned away and disappeared.

Did You Know?

● Was Mothman linked to an Indian's curse? The first encounter with Mothman was at Chief Cornstalk Hunting Ground, a park named for a Shawnee wrongly convicted of killing a settler. Shot by soldiers, the dying chief said "For this, may the curse of the Great Spirit rest upon this land."

● A carefully documented book on the Mothman was John Keel's 1975 volume, *The Mothman Prophecies*. This was made into a 2002 movie of the same name starring Richard Gere. It tells the story of the journalist Keel investigating the strange happenings, but the movie adds events to create more drama.

● Downtown Point Pleasant now has a spectacular statue of Mothman created by Robert Roach, a local sculptor. A plaque on its base says the Mothman legacy has "grown into a phenomenon known all over the world by millions of curious people." An annual Mothman Festival is held in its vicinity.

Where in the World?

The city of Point Pleasant, which has a population of more than 4,000, lies on the western edge of West Virginia, facing Ohio across the Ohio River. It is the county seat of scenic Mason County.

WEST VIRGINIA

Emela-ntouka

The violent-tempered Emela-ntouka is a beast that pygmies in the Congo supposedly fear more than any other. It is a plant-eater, but its name in the Lingala language means "killer of elephants," for this creature uses the sharp white horn on its snout to spear elephants and other animals that invade its territory in the impenetrable Likouala swamp. People often confuse it with the similar mythical Mokele-mbembe (see pp. 16–17). The fearful inhabitants of the region say Emela-ntouka is gray and resembles a rhinoceros, with smooth gray skin, short thick legs, and a heavy tail like a crocodile's. Some have heard the rough sound it makes, described as a growl or a snort. One belief is that Emela-ntouka is a surviving dinosaur, perhaps one of the horned-headed ceratopsians. Other investigators think it might be a new type of rhinoceros that can live in or near water.

▶ Elephants and other animals, such as buffalos and hippos, that wander into the irritable Emela-ntouka's homeland can expect a hostile reception. Natives have also had fearful encounters. The Emela-ntouka possesses the advantage of being a strong swimmer because of its powerful tail. Besides its swamp habitat, the creature has been sighted on firmer land. One suggestion is that it was once a prehistoric giant rhinoceros that evolved into an aquatic animal. Stories of the beast became more believable in 1954 when a former Likouala game inspector described it in the serious journal *Mammalia*, saying it was larger than a buffalo.

Where in the World?

The Congo Republic lies in west-central Africa between Gabon to the west and the much larger Congo on the east. Emela-ntouka have mostly been encountered in the large Likouala swamp in the country's northern region.

● CONGO REPUBLIC

Did You Know?

● The Emela-ntouka became widely known in 1933. The author J. E. Hughes reported that Wa-Ushi tribesmen killed one of the creatures, though he did not use its name. He described the animal's horn as being of smooth, polished white ivory and expressed regret that the natives had not kept it.

● The use of different names for Emela-ntouka has created difficulties. Some natives called the animal Chipekwe. As early as 1919, a London newspaper carried an account of a Chipekwe beast with a single ivory horn. Another group of natives said they observed the creature in Zaire and named it Irizima.

● Although the white horn of the Emela-ntouka looks like polished ivory, no one is certain what it consists of. Its dangerous horn, solid and strong enough to kill an elephant, is probably bone. This means the animal cannot be a rhinoceros, whose "horn" is actually a mass of hard hair.

Hopkinsville Goblins

A farmhouse battle against goblinlike men from a spaceship supposedly occurred near Hopkinsville, Kentucky, on the evening of August 21, 1955, and into the next morning. The event, also known as the Kelly-Hopkinsville Encounter, saw a family in the community of Kelly shoot at an estimated 12 to 15 little men who had landed in a flying saucer and approached the house. The invaders were about 4 feet (1.2 m) tall and had large heads with big eyes and long arms. Their silvery bodies glowed in the dark and floated. Two men in the house began shooting at the "goblins," but none seemed hurt. One invader even pulled the hair of a victim. The terrified family drove to nearby Hopkinsville to report the incident to police. Officers found evidence of the shooting at the house but nothing else. The family later reported that the spacemen returned and drew more gunfire before vanishing.

▶ A farmhouse being attacked by beings from a flying saucer is unlike any other UFO story. It began when a visiting friend went to fetch water from a well and observed a disk-shaped craft land nearby but making only a slight hissing noise. The terrified family said the initial siege lasted nearly four hours, with one of the goblin creatures in a tree and another on top of the house. The invaders seemed to tease the family by popping up outside different windows. When shots were fired and hit the aliens, the sound was like bullets banging against a metal bucket.

Where in the World?

The city of Hopkinsville, with a population of more than 28,000, is the county seat of Christian County in southwestern Kentucky. The Sutton farmhouse is about 8 miles (12.9 km) north in the small community of Kelly.

KENTUCKY

Did You Know?

• This reported UFO incident was seriously investigated by more than 20 police officers and the U.S. Air Force. One Hopkinsville policeman who had seen three flying saucers the previous year, said, "If I saw them, the Kelly story certainly could be true." No evidence of a hoax was ever uncovered.

• Some people have suggested that the "goblins" were actually great horned owls that live in the area. These large birds seem to float during the night and have big staring eyes. This theory, of course, fails to explain the eyewitness descriptions of the creatures' long arms and glowing silver-colored bodies.

• Cecil "Lucky" Sutton, the head of the family involved, never sold his story and, in fact, tried to avoid the limelight. When sightseers were drawn to the house, he eventually banned them from his property. Sutton stopped talking about the frightening event, but admitted that he thought about it constantly.

Gremlins

When your computer keeps crashing or your car engine regularly dies, are gremlins at work? This idea began as wartime humor, but many have come to believe that these gnomelike beings are responsible for unexplained mechanical failures. Gremlins became key suspects in World War II when British pilots accused them of sabotaging their planes during flights. These were mostly tongue-in-cheek comments, but some took them seriously. Returning pilots claimed to have seen tiny critters tinkering with their aircraft's equipment. One airman even found teeth marks on a cut cable, and as late as 1996 an Australian military pilot failed to mention his suspicions about gremlins in case "nice young men in clean white coats" took him away. Skeptics, however, believe that the stress of high-altitude air battles caused hallucinations of gremlins and their supernatural powers.

▶ The enemy was not the only danger facing British pilots, if their stories of gremlins were true. The critters were first reported by British pilots flying at high altitudes on photo reconnaissance missions. Aircraft mechanics, of course, liked the idea of putting the blame on gremlins. During World War II, it was assumed at first that the gremlins were working with the enemy, but unexplained accidents also occurred on German planes. Pilots were usually light-hearted about the creatures, inventing gremlin jokes, poems, and songs. Roald Dahl embellished the myth in his book, calling male gremlins "widgets" and female ones "fifinellas."

Where in the World?

Gremlins were first encountered in World War II by Royal Air Force pilots flying out of British air bases. The idea of misbehaving, plane-sabotaging gnomes quickly spread to military pilots from Canada, Australia, and the USA.

● GREAT BRITAIN

Did You Know?

● The British children's writer Roald Dahl popularized gremlins worldwide. He was a wartime pilot with the Royal Air Force who accidentally crashed. Dahl wrote *The Gremlins* while stationed in Washington, D.C., in 1943. Walt Disney planned to turn the book into a movie but never did. The book was republished in 2007.

● The 1984 movie *Gremlins* and its 1990 sequel took the mischievous characters into civilian life to cause havoc in neighborhood homes. This version introduces its own idea of green large-eared monsters with dangerous teeth and claws. Starting out as one cuddly pet, the creature turns into several destructive gremlin monsters.

● Nobody knows exactly how the gremlin name was chosen. In the 1920s British airmen used the term for men doing burdensome work. They may have combined "goblin" with the name of a popular drink, Fremlins. But the Irish also have used the Gaelic word "gruaimin" for an ill-humored little person.

Yowie

Australia's version of Bigfoot comes from Aboriginal myths dating back thousands of years. Their legends recount a final battle in which the apemen were defeated while fighting bare-handed against Aborigine weapons. European settlers first encountered the creature in 1881, originally calling it Yahoo and then Yowie. They described the monsters as terrifying, standing upright to 7 feet (2 m) with muscular bodies covered in gray hair. Its red eyes were deeply set, and the hands and feet (with four toes) were much larger than a human's. They ate any animal or human, snarling or screaming as they attacked. One researcher has collected 3,000 reports of Yowies. In 1997, for example, a woman living in Tanimi Desert was awakened by a horrible sound and watched a foul-smelling apeman rip down her fence as it fled, leaving behind giant footprints and a farm pipe it had chewed.

▶ Australia's stunning and solitary landscape has been the backdrop for much folklore, with few tales equaling the terror of Yowie. Aborigines said the creatures were too frightening to even look at, but they still regarded them as sacred beings from their "Dreamtime," when their first ancestors were created. The early European settlers believed the powerfully built Yowie were a giant race who lived in the continent's largely unexplored interior. All feared the apeman who avoided groups of people but targeted lone victims. Yowies would approach in slow, stalking movements before emitting blood-curling screams as they rushed in for the kill.

Where in the World?

Yowies prefer hiding in remote areas like mountains and dense forests. People have reported seeing them in every state of Australia, but mostly in New South Wales in the southeast and Queensland in the northeast.

NEW SOUTH WALES

Did You Know?

● An early confrontation with a Yowie took place in 1889 when men were moving cattle along a riverbank. Their dogs began whimpering and the cattle stampeded as the beast emerged from the forest waving a large tree limb. One rifleman wounded the Yowie, and it disappeared, screaming, into the woods.

● If the Yowie is a surviving prehistoric species, some investigators say he may be from Gigantopithecus, a large Asian ape that was up to 12 feet (3.7 m) tall and lived 8 million years ago. This ape existed alongside early species of humans who may have killed many and driven them into hiding.

● The Yowie's name probably comes from "youree," an Aborigine word for "the monster." Another Aboriginal name for the apeman is "Narcoonah," while their word for another of the Yowie's names, "Great Hairy Man," is "Doolagarl." The Yowie may be a species of "bunyip," the Aboriginal name for a monster living in local rivers and lakes.

Goatman

One of the oddest myths involves a monster that is half-man and half-goat. This savage creature has been sighted since 1957 in Prince George's County, Maryland, and more recently in Texas and about a dozen other states. Witnesses describe him as being up to 7 feet (2 m) tall with a horned head, the legs and hooves of a goat, and a hairy human torso. People have compared his features with the satyrs of Greek mythology, the Greek god Pan. The Goatman has a known hatred for people and animals, especially dogs and other pets, which he eats. He usually launches his attacks from the woods, by leaping into cars. He terrifies drivers and passengers by leaping onto the hood and waving a double-edged ax at them before disappearing into the trees.

► Morbid fear strikes those who encounter the rampaging Goatman waving his ax. Many of his victims have been youths parked in secluded spots, and this has prompted teenagers to gather on Friday and Saturday night vigils in the hope of catching sight of the grotesque beast. On one November evening in 1971, so many high school students came together that they blocked a road and police had to clear it. One truck carried students who claimed they had captured the elusive creature. Locals say they wouldn't be so brave if they could view the bodies of animals slain by the Goatman.

Where in the World?

The Goatman was first spotted in Maryland's Prince George's County, which borders Washington, D.C. Most Texas encounters have occurred in the east-central Waco area and around the town of Bowie, located north of Fort Worth.

MARYLAND ●

Did You Know?

● The Texas Goatman has often terrorized people in Bowie near Oklahoma. In 1971, residents heard strange noises at night and saw a creature running on two legs. The next morning a dog was found decapitated. Goatman hunters arrived in such great numbers that police had to clear them from the roads.

● A popular theory about the Goatman's origin is that he was a scientist working in a laboratory on experiments with goats that went wrong, turning him into a mutant goatlike creature. This caused him to go mad and flee into adjacent woods where he became murderous, taking revenge on normal humans.

● One bridge in Prince George's County in Maryland is nicknamed "Crybaby Bridge" because a depressed mother is supposed to have drowned her baby there. Today, in addition to this story, some locals say that drivers who stop on the bridge late in the night will often hear the horrible braying of the Goatman.

Jersey Devil

For the past 260 years, the state of New Jersey has been plagued by a monster described as a hideous mixture of several animals. The Jersey Devil, also known by its old name of Leeds Devil, is described as having a kangaroo body, dog head, horse face and hooves, bat wings, and a forked tail. It has red eyes that glow with an intensity that can paralyze a person. Farmers have said that it killed their animals and caused crops to fail. In 1909 so many sightings were reported that officials in those areas closed schools and factories. Some people even believed the Jersey Devil's appearance meant a great tragedy was about to occur because he was sighted just before the American Revolution and the Civil War. Although the creature is still seen, locals are now proud of their monster, whose name is worn by the New Jersey Devils professional hockey team.

▶ Rewards for capturing the elusive Jersey Devil have little chance of being collected. Sightings have become fewer, although a woman reported in 2007 a "gargoylelike creature" with bat wings perched in a tree. Police have not handled an official case for more than 30 years. The myth has been kept alive, however, in books, articles, and television programs, including *The X-Files*. Tourist stores near the Pine Barrens in southern New Jersey, the monster's home territory, also offer Jersey Devil souvenirs like pennants and bumper stickers. In Winslow Township, one merchant charges $1 to view the alleged skull of the beast.

Where in the World?

The Jersey Devil lives in southern New Jersey in the Pine Barrens, also known as the Pinelands. This area of thick forest is a short drive from Atlantic City. The Garden State Parkway crosses the area.

NEW JERSEY ●

Did You Know?

● Legend has it that the creature was first called the Leeds Devil because of a poor woman, Mother Leeds. One version says she gave birth in the 1730s to her thirteenth child and abandoned it in the woods. The infant was so furious at being rejected that it grew into the monster.

● The Jersey Devil was reportedly shot with a cannon in the early nineteenth century. Commodore Stephen Decatur was testing cannonballs when he spied the frightening animal flying by. He turned a cannon to the heavens and made a direct hit on the creature's wing, but the monster flew leisurely away.

● Reports in 1909 indicated that the Jersey Devil was attracted to trolley cars. Several towns began carrying armed guards on board after the creature attacked one of the vehicles. In another incident, it landed on an electric rail in the town of Clayton but flew off with no apparent injury.

Onza

Some believe that the ferocious onza is a mythical species, but the large wildcat has been recorded since the Spanish conquistadors invaded Mexico. They found some in the zoo of Emperor Montezuma under the Aztec name of "cuitlamiztli" and saw onzas in the wild, where they attacked people more often than other big cats. Spanish missionaries wrote about attacks on children and the death of a soldier. The onza's home is mainly in Mexico, but modern sightings have also occurred throughout Central and South America. Experts say the animal might be a subspecies of a puma or cougar, but the onza is smaller and thinner, with longer, wolflike ears. It has similarities to a cheetah, with nonretractable claws and a similar method of springing. A German scientist suggests the onza may be a living specimen of a prehistoric American cheetah, but others believe it is a distinct species.

▶ Ancient Aztec carvings highlight the mythical face of the onza. Spanish conquistadors gave the wild cat its name based on the Latin term for a cheetah. One conquistador wrote that the Aztec zoo had three types of large cats, and described the onza as resembling a "wolf-cat." Most recorded accounts of sightings ended in the middle of the eighteenth century and few were noted for about 170 years. Interest returned in 1938 when three Americans hunting in the Mexican state of Sinaloa killed a strange cat that resembled a lighter puma but had longer legs, ears, and body. Locals identified it as an onza.

Where in the World?

The onza lives mostly in the mountains of northwestern Mexico, often seen in the state of Sinaloa facing the Gulf of California. Other sightings are in Central America, such as northern Guatemala, and South America.

● SINALOA

Did You Know?

● Researchers at Texas Tech University examined a frozen big cat said to be an onza in 1998. They verified that it was an onza, but decided the animal is probably a subspecies of a cougar rather than a new species. They also left open the possibility that the onza may even be a mutant cougar.

● Christopher Columbus wrote to the Spanish king about a hunter shooting an arrow to kill "a beast like a cat, but pretty much longer and with a humanlike face." Even as the animal was dying, Columbus added, it attacked a wild boar and used its leg to strangle it.

● An onza was shot in 1986 by a Mexican rancher who thought it was a jaguar about to attack him while he was hunting deer with a friend. He showed it to another hunter who identified it as the same type of animal his father had killed a decade earlier.

Beast of Bodmin Moor

Have large wildcats prowled a desolate part of Britain for more than 40 years? Farmers on Bodmin Moor in Cornwall who have found their livestock savaged by unknown predators believe so. Their fears were reinforced by photographs and video footage of pantherlike cats roaming the brooding landscape. One captured image showed a black animal about 3 feet 6 inches (1 m) long. Press coverage of these images and of the mauled livestock helped launch an investigation in 1995 by the government's agriculture ministry. It found "no verifiable evidence" that the creatures existed, but also had no proof that big cats were not on the moor. Locals still speculate about what was seen on film. Some believe the creature is a species of wildcat supposedly extinct for more than a century in Britain. Others suggest they were imported animals that had escaped from private zoos.

▶ The sharp-toothed skull of a big cat discovered in 1995 convinced many locals that a beast roamed among them. Missing its lower jaw, the skull measured 7 inches (18 cm) long and 4 inches (10 cm) wide. Investigators said it was probably from a leopardskin rug. Inside the skull was an egg case of a tropical cockroach that couldn't live in Britain. This was another setback for farmers convinced that a big cat was killing their livestock. Their member of parliament summed up their feelings by saying that those who had seen the beast "did not take kindly to being portrayed as gullible yokels."

Where in the World?

Bodmin Moor, comprising 80 square miles (207 sq km) of granite uplands, is in the northern region of Cornwall. That county occupies the extreme southwestern peninsula of England between the Atlantic Ocean and the English Channel.

● CORNWALL

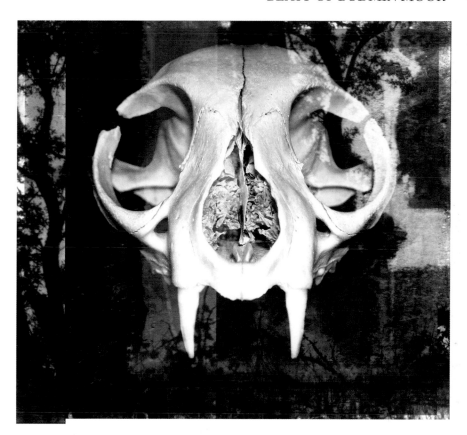

Did You Know?

● In 1999 a squadron of Cornish reserves from the Royal Air Force spent a night on Bodmin Moor with the latest military night-vision equipment to observe the legendary "beast." The volunteers camped under hedges and in ditches, but poor weather ruined their efforts. The devices did pick up some unidentifiable movements, however.

● Days after the government's official report, a 14-year-old boy found the skull of a big cat that had sharp incisors. This was given to the Natural History Museum in London, which said it was from a male leopard from India but had knife cuts normally used for a leopardskin rug.

● Bodmin Moor, where people have lived since 10,000 B.C.E., has many mysterious connections. Legendary King Arthur may have traveled through the area from his home, Camelot, which many believe was in Cornwall. The moor also has strange stone circles and rows left from the Bronze Age that have inspired other legends.

Chupacabra

One of the strangest vampire creatures is the Chupacabra, in both humanoid and canine forms. It attacks animals, draining their bodies of blood. Chupacabra is roughly translated as "goat sucker," but it has killed everything from birds to horses. First known in Puerto Rico in 1995 when 1,000 mysterious animal deaths were recorded, the monster now ranges through several U.S. states, including California, Texas, New Mexico, and Maine, as well as Mexico, Brazil, and other Latin American countries. Eyewitnesses describe most Chupacabras as being lizardlike humanoids standing 3 feet (1 m) or more that screech and are able to hop some 20 feet (6 m). Its other guise has a hairless body, doglike face, large fangs, forked tongue, and glowing red hypnotic eyes that can paralyze. Among the many theories is that the Chupacabra is a genetic mutant or an extraterrestrial.

▶ The vampire "goat sucker" is a menace to any animal it can overpower. One of the first reported attacks, in 1995 in Puerto Rico, left eight sheep dead, each with puncture wounds in the chest and no blood in the body. Other countries soon blamed Chupacabra for vampire killings. In Columbia, some believe the goat sucker is the same as their mythical creature called the "mosquito man," who sucks an animal's blood through his lengthy nose. The Chupacabra name has spread from a single Puerto Rican source, Silverio Perez, a comedian and television star who coined it as a joke.

Where in the World?

Chupacabras come from Puerto Rico, an island of the West Indies and a self-governing part of the United States. These vampires have also ranged from the U.S. state of Maine to Brazil in South America.

PUERTO RICO

Did You Know?

• In 2005, a research team spent eight months in South American jungles to prove that Chupacabra exists. The $6 million project was able to film an unknown creature and collect hair and skin samples. These were given to the University of Texas, where scientists were unable to match them to any known species.

• A rancher in south Texas found a dead animal in 2007 and said it was a chupacabra, though other people thought it was a fox or coyote. Phylis Canion said it had snatched her cats and killed two dozen chickens, pulling their heads off and sucking all the blood out.

• Chupacabras are even now being spotted far away from the Americas. Farmers in central Russia reported in 2005 that one of the terrifying creatures had killed 32 of their turkeys and drained their blood, while another incident in the region involved 30 dead sheep whose bodies were also sucked dry.

Kongamato

If the pterosaur, a prehistoric flying reptile, could still live, it might be the kongamato, which sometimes appears from the deep swamps and brush of south-central Africa. It seems incredible we could see a creature that existed 65 million years ago, but natives have identified the pterosaur in books as being the exact image of kongamato. The name means "overwhelmer of boats," for kongamatos are ferocious, capsizing light boats and attacking people. Several deaths have been attributed to their long, sharp beaks. The creatures are said to eat decomposing human flesh, digging up bodies in shallow graves. Some natives once carried charms to protect them from the beasts. The kongamato is red or black with leathery batlike wings and a narrow head with a beak full of pointed teeth. Its wingspan has been estimated at 3 to 7 feet (1 to 2 m) and its length at 4 feet 6 inches (1.4 m).

▶ Colorful carvings and paintings by natives add to the story of the dreadful kongamato. In his 1932 book on Africa, the explorer Frank Welland said natives described the creature as looking exactly like a pterodactyl. He added that they did not consider kongamato to be an unnatural thing like a demon, "only a very awful thing, like a man-eating lion or a rogue elephant, but infinitely worse." Once when the zoologist and explorer Ivan T. Sanderson pointed out the direction of his apparent sighting of kongamato, his native guides fled in fear the opposite way, leaving their personal valuables behind.

Where in the World?

The border area of Zambia, Congo, and Angola in south-central Africa is a reputed haunt of kongamatos. They have often been seen in Jiundu Swamp in northwestern Zambia and even near Mount Kilimanjaro in Tanzania.

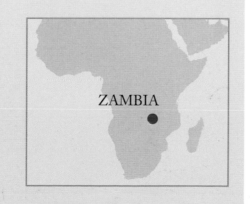

ZAMBIA

Did You Know?

• A British Museum expedition in 1932–33 explored West Africa and had a dramatic encounter with kongamatos in the Cameroons. The zoologist Ivan T. Sanderson fell into a river and was suddenly attacked by one. The explorer dived safely underwater and later reported the creature had "great, black, dracula-like wings."

• In 1957 a patient arrived at a hospital in Zambia with a severe chest wound and reported that a giant bird had attacked him. Officials asked him to draw a picture of the creature, and his drawing resembled a pterosaur. Mysterious flying creatures had been seen there a year before.

• Native peoples in Northern Rhodesia (now Zambia) once believed they would die if they looked at a kongamato. In 1942, they told the explorer Captain Charles R. S. Pitman that death was assured by viewing the beast, which, he described, was "on a gigantic scale strangely reminiscent of the prehistoric pterodactyl."

Ropen

Like Africa's kongamato, the ropen of Papua New Guinea has been called a pterosaur, a living prehistoric animal. The ropen, however, has the specialized ability to emit a yellowish glow at intervals of five to six seconds as it flies. The natives call these lights "indava." The animal uses this bioluminescence to attract fish and other sea life to the surface at night to supply its main diet. It also dines on dead animals and has appeared at funerals seeking the remains of the departed. Several ropens live on the mainland, where they occasionally attack humans, and an older peaceful one inhabits Umboi Island. A dark gray or brown nocturnal creature, the ropen has a long beak with sharp teeth, a snakelike neck, leathery batlike wings with a span up to 20 feet (6 m), and a long tail. Bumps run from the back of the head to the tail.

▶ Capturing a flying ropen on film may be a futile task, but people still try, and have been encouraged by Paul Nation's videotape in 2006 of two indava lights. These glowing spots are the main evidence of the mostly nocturnal creature as it flies swifter than birds over land. Photographers would be lucky to catch the ropen resting against the truck of a tree because eyewitnesses say that it latches onto the trunk in an upright position like a woodpecker. Jonathan Whitcomb, a forensic videographer, collected details of the ropen's habits in his book *Searching for Ropens*, which was published in 2007.

Where in the World?

Papua New Guinea is situated in the Pacific Ocean in Southeast Asia. It occupies half of the island of New Guinea and some 600 islands. Umboi Island is located between the mainland and the large New Britain Island.

PAPUA NEW GUINEA

Did You Know?

• A Texan named Paul Nation videotaped the indava lights while exploring mountains in Papua New Guinea. They seemed to come from Umboi Island. This video was viewed by several experts, including a missile defense physicist, and all said the lights could not be identified as coming from any known object.

• One of the most credible sightings of a ropen was by Duane Hodgkinson, who was stationed in New Guinea during World War II. As he and another military man walked through a clearing in 1944, they were amazed when a ropen suddenly flew straight up into the air and circled.

• The tail of the ropen is inflexible and only moves where it connects to the body. Natives on the north-central part of Umboi Island say the creature always keeps its tail straight. This is a feature found on fossils of pterosaurs, with movement restricted only to the vertebrae at the tail's base.

Orang Bati

Surely nothing is more hideous than a monster that eats children. Yet this is what the islanders of Seram in Indonesia have faced with the dreaded Orang Bati since the fifteenth century. Locals say this giant flying creature has raided villages at night to abduct infants and children, carrying the victims away to its home in Mount Kairatu, an extinct volcano, to devour them. Known as "the winged man," Orang Bati resembles a human or giant ape that stands up to 5 feet (1.5 m) tall. Its reddish skin contrasts with its large leathery batlike wings, which are sometimes covered with dense black fur. Its long thin tail is similar to that of a flying pterosaur. Adding to the terror is the animal's wail, which is long, shrill, and mournful. Some believe Orang Bati may be a flying primate, the first ever discovered, or a monkey-eating bat that has decided to prey on children.

▶ The idea of a flying creature that is half-man and half-bat is bizarre, but this is a frequent description of Orang Bati. Missionaries on Seram as long ago as the fifteenth century were told about the winged animal, whose night raids terrorized the village of Uraur. Virtually all of the descriptions of the beast have been oral accounts by natives. The sighting by the missionary Tyson Hughes is the only one documented, and no physical evidence has ever been recovered. Those investigating the Orang Bati have pointed out its similarities to the kongamato of Africa and the ropen of Papua New Guinea.

Did You Know?

● One English man who became a believer in Orang Bati was the missionary Tyson Hughes. He lived among the people of Maluku for 18 months, beginning in 1987, to help them with their farming methods. At first skeptical about tales of a flying beast, Hughes was stunned halfway through his mission when he encountered one.

● The Orang Bati has also been sighted on other Indonesian islands, but has never seized children. Another similar animal is the ahool that lives in Java, but natives assume it is just a giant bat. The Philippines have also reported giant bats that swoop into villages to kill livestock.

● Mount Kairatu, home of Orang Bati, is Seram's dormant volcano in the center of the island. It has a network of very deep caves in which the creature hides during the daytime. This region is packed with mountain ranges and dense rainforests that have seldom been explored.

Where in the World?

Seram is the second largest of the Maluku "spice islands," an archipelago in the eastern region of Indonesia. This is a cluster of some 1,000 islands located at the equator west of New Guinea.

SERAM

Stockholm Metro Ghost Train

Sweden's capital city has one of the most haunted subway systems in the world. Users of the Stockholm Metro swap many stories about its ghost train, ghost riders, and even a ghost station. The Silverpilen, which means "Silver Arrow," is an eight-car train that was built in the 1960s as a test model using C5 silver cars. All other cars are green or blue. Even though it has long been out of service, the gleaming ghost train is still seen by the city's residents after midnight as it streaks nonstop through stations. Subway workers say they have encountered it in abandoned tunnels. More worrying are tales of the train stopping unexpectedly to pick up passengers who then disembark up to a year later or who are never seen again. One well-known incident is of a young woman who disappeared after boarding the Silverpilen at midnight and was later found dead in nearby woods.

▶ The beautiful city of Stockholm has a menacing phantom beneath its streets, according to a persistent rumor. Sometimes the Silverpilen speeds empty through the depths and on other journeys it is transporting ghostly passengers whose dead faces stare out of the windows. Even during the train's short life to test new cars, it was seldom seen. The ghost stories began to circulate widely in the 1980s and were featured on Swedish television in 1997 in a program investigating realistic ghost sightings. Some people still avoid the subway during its midnight travels or check carefully for ghostly visions and sounds in the tunnels.

Where in the World?

Stockholm, Sweden's largest city, has a port located on the Baltic Sea on the eastern coast of Sweden, in the Scandinavian Peninsula in northern Europe. The city's vast area covers the mainland and many adjacent islands.

● STOCKHOLM

Did You Know?

● Stockholm's ghost station is called Kymlinge. It was built in the early 1970s but it never opened because locals protested that it would ruin their green area. The Silverpilen ghost train is supposed to disembark any passengers there, and people now have a saying that "Only the dead get off at Kymlinge."

● The Stockholm Metro has 100 stations. The three lines are named after colors. The Green opened in 1950, the Red in 1964, and the Blue in 1975. The most recent station was opened in 1994. The stations are known as "the longest art gallery in the world" because of their colorful decorations.

● When the Silverpilen train rushes through the desolated and spookily quiet stations, it produces a screeching wail that echoes through the tunnels. This is the mechanical noise made along the rails during its original tests. The ghostly sounds are often accompanied by a chilly wind flowing with the ghost train.

Crew of the *Mary Celeste*

One of the greatest ghost ships of all time, the *Mary Celeste* was discovered on December 4, 1871, under sail drifting in the Atlantic Ocean with nobody on board. Missing and never found were Captain Benjamin Briggs, his wife and two-year-old daughter, and the ship's crew of eight. The *Mary Celeste* had set sail from New York with cargo destined for Genoa, Italy. Its log was found and the final entry on November 25, 1871, indicated it had sailed some 500 miles (805 km) from its last recorded position in the Azores. The compass was destroyed, the hatch covers had been blown off, and the lifeboat was missing. Some believed the ship was cursed, and others suggested a giant squid had devoured everyone on board. A more realistic theory is that there was an explosion and so the captain launched the lifeboat, which sank in the rough sea.

▶ The first view of the ghost ship from the bows of the *Dei Gratia* struck fear into the hearts of its crew. A small boat was used to board the *Mary Celeste*, and the first mate, Oliver Deveau, found the ship in fairly good condition but "a thoroughly wet mess." He captained the stricken vessel to Gibraltar and used its slate log to make new entries, accidentally erasing some of the older information. It was later suggested that pirates had boarded the *Mary Celeste* and killed everyone, but no pirate attacks had happened in the area for about 40 years.

Did You Know?

● The ship was a half-brigantine built in Nova Scotia, Canada, and launched in 1861 as *The Amazon*. Its bad luck included a collision in the English Channel, and then being beached in Nova Scotia during a storm in 1867. Two years later Americans bought the vessel and renamed her *Mary Celeste*.

● Several unproven rumors circulated after the ship was found. One said the crew had killed the captain after he caught them stealing. Other unlikely stories said a cat was found sleeping on a bunk and fresh food was on the table.

● The *Mary Celeste* was discovered by the crew of the *Dei Gratia*, which had left New York one week later. Three of the crew of *Dei Gratia* took command of the *Mary Celeste* and sailed it to Gibraltar, where they were first suspected of murder before being awarded salvage fees.

Where in the World?

The *Mary Celeste* was discovered 500 miles southeast of the Azores Islands, which lie 740 miles (1,191 km) west of Portugal. The ship was drifting toward the Strait of Gibraltar, which leads into the Mediterranean Sea.

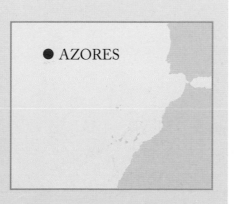

● AZORES

Ghost Prisoners of Alcatraz

Alcatraz, the former top-security prison in San Francisco Bay, is one of America's most haunted places. Park Service personnel, now in charge of "the Rock," have reported dreadful screams, sobbing, running footsteps, clanging cell doors, and rattling chains. Most haunted is the notorious D-Block, where the worst prisoners were isolated. Some officers refuse to enter the area alone because of the cold chills, eerie feelings, and strong vibrations in the cells. Another haunted area is the corridor where three inmates were riddled with bullets after killing two guards in an escape attempt in 1946. Security men have since seen apparitions of the dead guards and heard mysterious clanging noises along the corridor. Equally mysterious have been several incidents of guards being driven out of the laundry room by thick black smoke but returning minutes later to find no trace of smoke in the room.

▶ The strumming of banjo strings continues to echo through the deserted cells and corridors of Alcatraz. Al Capone's ghostly music is a chilling reminder of the years he spent in B-Block in ill health. A member of the prison band, he practiced his music in the shower room during recreational time, because he was frightened he would be murdered by inmates in the yard. "Scarface" had made many tough enemies during his gangster years in Chicago. Federal agents never could gather enough evidence about the murders he arranged, so Capone was imprisoned from 1931 to 1939 only for tax evasion.

Where in the World?

Alcatraz is situated on a rocky island in the middle of San Francisco Bay facing the city. San Francisco is a seaport in northern California on a peninsula separating the bay from the Pacific Ocean.

● SAN FRANCISCO

Did You Know?

● Al Capone, the infamous gangster who was interned in Alcatraz, learned to play the banjo while an inmate, usually practicing in the shower room. Recently, a park ranger who had no knowledge of this heard the sound of banjo music in that area. Others have also reported hearing banjo playing within the prison.

● James A. Johnston, warden during the 1946 escape attempt, was a man who did not believe in spirits. Yet he experienced a ghostly encounter when he was giving a tour of the facility. Sobs and other strange sounds rose within the walls and a chilly wind swept past the group.

● In the 1940s, a prisoner locked in cell 14D, an isolated "hole," screamed all through the night that someone with glowing eyes was killing him. The next morning, guards discovered him strangled to death, yet it was reported that he was later seen for a brief second standing in line with other convicts.

Crybaby Bridge

The urban myth of the haunted Crybaby Bridge has spread to bridges throughout the United States, but most are found in Ohio. The usual story says that a mother threw her unwanted baby off the bridge and that its cries can still be heard today. However, many local versions have developed in Ohio. At Rogue's Hollow near Doylestown, locals say a young mother accidentally drove off the bridge and her baby drowned in the freezing water. Days later, the grief-stricken woman returned to the bridge and leaped to her death. Both their cries can be heard at night. A different story is told in Salem, where a couple having an argument suddenly saw their baby fall from the bridge. People today claim they can hear the baby's cries and the mother's screams. Shelby's Crybaby Bridge involves the murder of an entire family, but only the cries of the infant can be heard.

▶ Infants have died in waters under bridges in many states, and this local story says their cries still linger on. People living nearby, particularly teenagers, usually drive to the death sites at night, with Halloween night being a popular time for visits. The myth has been weakened because its details are so similar at the different locations. When stories of various Crybaby Bridges began to appear on the Internet in 1999, the Maryland folklore expert Jesse Glass disputed them. He said the online versions were fakes because the tales were not known in folklore and regional newspapers had never mentioned such events.

Where in the World?

Ohio is a Midwestern state. Abbeyville and Shelby are in the north, Salem is in the east, Chillicothe is in the south, and Doylestown is in the northeast. Maryland is a Mid-Atlantic state and Bowie lies 12 miles (19 km) from Washington, D.C.

OHIO ●

Did You Know?

● Some communities have changed the story from a bridge to a tunnel. In Chillicothe, Ohio, people say a mother was crossing through a tunnel with her baby when a train entered and killed them both. Locals report that not only can they hear the child's cries but they can see the woman walking slowly through the tunnel.

● Maryland is among the several states with Crybaby Bridges. One near Bowie is a steel bridge where a mother and her infant were murdered. People parking there late at night report the baby's cries and have seen a ghost car approaching from behind but disappearing when you turn around to look at it.

● The Crybaby Bridge in Abbeyville, Ohio, can even affect your car. An unmarried woman gave birth in the 1950s and threw the baby from the bridge. Anyone now visiting the spot can hear the baby but they dare not turn off their car's engine because it will not start again.

The Monster of Glamis Castle

Glamis Castle is said to be the most haunted castle in Scotland. One of its saddest stories concerns a hideously deformed family member who was locked up his entire life in a secret room measuring only 10 by 15 feet (3 by 4.6 m). Outsiders were told he had died within days of birth—otherwise this first-born son would have inherited the castle. The "monster" was Thomas Bowes-Lyon, who should have become Lord Glamis. He was described as being "an enormous flabby egg" because his hairy deformed body lacked a neck and had tiny limbs. A trusted servant pushed his meals through an iron grate in his door and is said to have walked him along the battlements on dark nights (one is still named the Mad Earl's Walk). Rumors said he was exceptionally strong and lived for more than 100 years. Nobody knows how he died, and no tombstone marks his grave.

▶ A boarded door concealed the awful secret within the splendid Glamis Castle. Another ghost is that of the fifteenth century Lord of Glamis, who refused to stop playing cards when the Sabbath arrived and is now doomed to play forever in a secret room. Also often seen is the ghost of a small boy who sits on a stone seat. Castle historians believe this is the spirit of an eighteenth-century servant boy who had been badly treated. An unknown ghost is a woman with no tongue who looks out from a barred window of the castle.

Where in the World?

Glamis Castle is situated in the Angus region of east Scotland on the North Sea. It is located outside the village of Glamis, south of the town of Forfar and north of the city of Dundee.

● GLAMIS

Did You Know?

● One of the ghosts seen in Glamis Castle is the "gray lady" who haunts the family chapel and appears over the clock tower. She is thought to be the Sixth Lady of Glamis who was burned at the stake in 1537, accused of being a witch and plotting to poison the king.

● The construction of Glamis Castle began in 1500. Visitors have included Mary Queen of Scots in 1562 and Shakespeare in 1599, who supposedly used it as the setting for his famous play *Macbeth*. It was the childhood home of the late Elizabeth, who became the Queen Mother, and the birthplace of her daughter, the late Princess Margaret, sister of Queen Elizabeth II.

● In the early 1900s, a workman accidentally broke through a wall into a passage that led to the secret room. He explored the dismal chamber and became deeply distressed. After questioning the workman, the earl stopped his renovation work and paid him thousands of pounds to keep silent and to emigrate to Australia.

The Hookerman's Light

A tragic railroad accident lies behind the legend of the Hookerman's Light. Back in the early days of train travel, the hookerman checked the rails for gaps and other problems. One man was doing the night shift with a lantern at Budd Lake, New Jersey, confident that no train was due. This was a fatal mistake. One suddenly roared into view just as he caught his hand under a rail. The engineer never saw the hookerman or his faint light, and in seconds the locomotive had torn off his arm and hand, still clutching the lantern. The poor man died of blood loss and shock, and his body was discovered the next morning. Since then, many people have seen the eerie flickering light hovering over the tracks, swinging from side to side. Some believe this is the Hookerman's Light as the man's missing arm hunts endlessly for his body.

▶ The train that bore down on the hookerman was probably carrying coal. The horrific accident became such a legend that scores of people, mostly teenagers, would gather at certain points along the track in the 1970s and had to be dispersed by the police. Those who still make the trip usually watch along a stretch of the High Bridge Railroad, which is now closed. Official railroad documents do report that such an accident happened in that area during the nineteenth century. Warnings continue to be made that the hookerman's arm wants to search alone for its body and will chase anybody else away.

Where in the World?

The Hookerman's Light is seen close to the accident site on a disused stretch of the High Bridge Railroad. This old line runs through Long Valley and Flanders in the northern region of New Jersey.

NEW JERSEY ●

Did You Know?

● A faint light does glow over the tracks where the accident occurred. This has been explained as coming from chemicals in the soil or from reflections of other light sources. However, such a practical explanation hardly satisfies those who drive out at night to view the mysterious light over the tracks.

● The myth of the Hookerman's Light has proven to have a commercial value. There is a drink called the "Hookerman's Light." The drink company is located in a restored 200-year-old barn at the foot of Schooley's Mountain not far from the place where the unfortunate rail worker died.

● The hookerman legend may be related to another accident that occurred nearby in the late 1800s. A conductor fell from his train as it departed and wounded his arm badly. The train sped him to the area of a doctor's house. His life was saved but his arm was lost.

The Hampton Court Ghosts

Hampton Court Palace in London is awash with age-old mysteries, and is said to be haunted by two of King Henry VIII's six wives. Most seen is his fifth wife, Catherine Howard, whom he had executed in 1542. She was dragged away screaming by soldiers through an area now called the Haunted Gallery. Visitors, staff, and workmen have encountered her ghost and heard her desperate cries. Henry's third and favorite wife, Jane Seymour, died in the palace, and her ghost has been viewed wandering around the Clock Court. In 2003, a security camera picked up doors opening in the palace with no one there, then a vision of a woman wearing a full cloak appeared and closed them. The face did not look human, and the staff have never found a rational explanation. Visitors to Hampton Court have also experienced cold feelings, and some have fainted.

▶ The beheading of Queen Catherine Howard created one of Britain's most popular ghost stories. As she was dragged from the palace, people could hear Catherine's terrible cries that she had to see the king and beg him to drop the charges against her. She was executed on February 13, 1542, only two years after their marriage. In 2001, a team led by Dr. Richard Wiseman of Hertfordshire University hunted for Catherine's ghost. They set up thermal cameras and air movement detectors along the 20-yard (18-m) Haunted Gallery, but the special devices only detected a cleaning woman carrying a vacuum cleaner.

Where in the World?

Hampton Court Palace is situated in the suburban borough of Richmond in southwest London, England. The famous building stands on the banks of the Thames River, being 14 miles (23 km) upstream from the main city.

LONDON ●

Did You Know?

● Hampton Court Palace offered guided two-hour evening ghost tours in 2008. Advertisements called it "a truly spine-chilling experience." Visitors were charged £25 (about $50) to view the most haunted rooms, which are normally off-limits to tourists. Anyone under the age of 12 was not allowed in such spooky chambers.

● Henry VIII spent ten years rebuilding and extending Hampton Court, finishing in about 1540. He added tennis courts, bowling alleys, a chapel, pleasure gardens, and a hunting park. All of his six wives came to the palace. When he died, it was the most lavish of his more than 60 houses.

● So many people reported seeing Catherine Howard's ghost in the Haunted Gallery that Hampton Court's authorities called in ghost-busting psychologists. They interviewed some 400 palace visitors who had felt a ghostly presence, but the team decided the tourists' sudden feelings of coldness were due to drafts in the old building.

Bermuda Triangle

One of the greatest mysteries of the twentieth century lies in the Atlantic Ocean. The Bermuda Triangle is an area enclosed by imaginary lines framing the vast graveyard of many missing ships and aircraft. They disappeared for unknown reasons and have never been found. Among the most mysterious is the 1945 loss of Flight 19—five U.S. bombers that departed from Fort Lauderdale, Florida. The weather conditions were average, but the planes' compasses began to experience malfunctions and then lost radio contact. Flight 19 was never heard from again and no trace of the planes was ever found. Equally eerie was the 1918 disappearance of the USS *Cyclops*. After sailing to Brazilian waters to fuel British ships in World War I, she put to sea from Rio de Janeiro, reached Barbados, and was never heard from again, her 306 crew and passengers disappearing without a trace.

▶ Sometimes known as the "Devil's Triangle," the area combines heavy shipping traffic with some tempestuous weather, including raging thunderstorms. Most of the mysterious disappearances have been on the Triangle's southern boundary, which takes in the Bahamas and the Florida Straits. There are usually no witnesses to a sinking or crash in this vast sea. Until the nineteenth century, the Triangle was one of the few places where a compass pointed toward true north instead of magnetic north. This once endangered ships by drawing them far off course, but changes in the Earth's magnetic field have now eliminated the problem.

Did You Know?

- Military and commercial organizations remain skeptical of paranormal aspects of the Bermuda Triangle. The U.S. Navy does not believe the doomed area exists, and Lloyd's of London, the shipping insurer, does not raise rates for vessels crossing the triangle. The busy shipping lane probably has a normal percentage of disappearances.

- A number of natural explanations have been offered for the disappearances. Strong currents over reefs in the area can cause navigational hazards, and freak waves, turbulent storms, and water spouts add special dangers. After a disaster, the rapid Gulf Stream is so strong it can erase any wreckage at sea.

- The first person to note odd happenings in the triangle was Christopher Columbus. In his log book on October 11, 1492, he recorded a distant light dancing up and down on the water "like the light of a wax candle." Another entry tells of strange compass bearings in the area.

Where in the World?

The Bermuda Triangle lies in the Atlantic Ocean off the southeastern coast of the United States. The boundaries are not official but are said to reach from Florida to San Juan, Puerto Rico, to Bermuda.

THE BERMUDA TRIANGLE

Spontaneous Human Combustion

Can people be burned to death by a fire starting from within their own body? This idea is called spontaneous human combustion, and hundreds of cases have been recorded since the seventeenth century. The victims apparently caught on fire from a chemical reaction within because no external ignition source was discovered. Often their limbs have no burns. Equally strange is that nothing else in the room is charred and sometimes not even their clothes. Explanations of spontaneous human combustion include the idea that static electricity can build up in the body and ignite the clothes. Scientists have doubted the whole thing, saying fires can burn in unusual ways and investigators often fail to find the real cause. They also point to the wick effect, when the burning body fat of a victim goes into the clothes and, like candle wax, keeps the flames away from other objects.

▶ Spontaneous human combustion is always unexpected, because it needs an intensely high heat not found in bodies. It would be a terrible death in which the victim feels a sudden boiling fire deep in their body. This would often be followed by flames bursting out on exposed areas like the hands and face. The person's clothes, according to the wick effect, would keep most flames inside, producing the charred remains that investigators have discovered. The fire's limited outlet keeps the surroundings, such as a room, from burning. The combustion process will often leave a sweet smoky odor in a room.

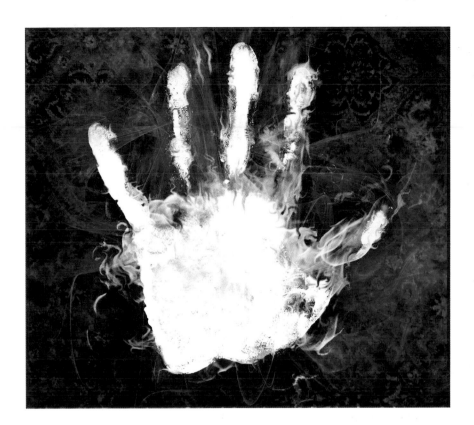

Where in the World?

Cases of spontaneous human combustion have occurred worldwide. The first incident was recorded in Paris in 1673, and nineteenth-century London had constant reports. Britain and the United States have had infrequent cases in modern times.

● PARIS

Did You Know?

● Although scientists reject the idea of a human bursting into flames spontaneously because of a chemical reaction, some objects do. Potassium is one material that suddenly ignites when contacting air or oxygen. Even oily rags in a bucket can burst into fire when exposed to air for a long period.

● A case of spontaneous human combustion in 1951 involved Mrs. Mary H. Reeser, 67, of St. Petersburg, Florida. Her burned body was found in a chair, but only her head shrunken to the size of an orange and her backbone and one foot remained. Her apartment showed no evidence of fire.

● Some cases of supposed spontaneous human combustion have involved only burns on the skin without any evidence of flames in the body. Others have reported that smoke escaped from their bodies without a fire, or that their clothes caught on fire without an apparent cause.

The Face on Mars

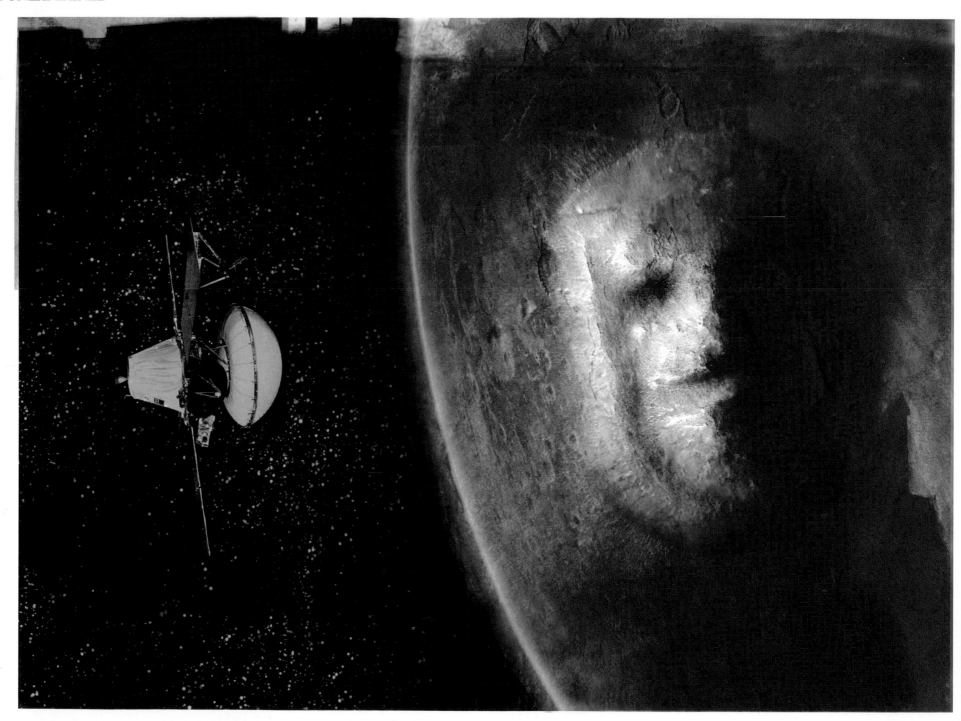

On July 25, 1976, when NASA's space probe *Viking Orbiter 1* was photographing the surface of Mars, "something funny happened," according to the agency. All of a sudden, controllers at the Jet Propulsion Lab saw a face nearly 2 miles (3.2 km) long appear on their monitors. NASA officials were amused, and released the photos to the public. One result, however, was an urban myth that the face had been artificially made by someone, and this indicated an ancient civilization had existed on the Red Planet. The space agency explained that the face was just a huge rock formation with shadows giving an illusion of an eyes, nose, and mouth. Still, so much mystery remained, NASA targeted the face again when Mars Global Surveyor arrived there in 1997 able to take pictures ten times sharper. These proved the face was made of buttes or mesas like those in the American West.

▶ Like a sleeping giant, the rust-tinted face on Mars provided some fun for NASA and created a legend that has now continued for more than 30 years. The story has appeared in magazines, books, and a movie, and has even been discussed on talk shows. NASA itself noted that the combination of rocks and shadows created a striking image resembling an Egyptian pharaoh. It said when other 3D elevation photos were taken from angles that had no shadows, the formation's eyes, nose, and mouth disappeared. NASA also noted that it would help the agency's budget if there *had* been an ancient civilization on Mars.

Where in the World?

Mars, of course, is not in the world, being 141.6 million miles (227.8 million km) from the Sun. It is the fifth planet and has an orbit next to, and outside, that of the Earth's.

Did You Know?

● Some rocks of the face are 800 feet (244 m) high. NASA published tongue-in-cheek suggestions for bold walkers on Mars. The distance would be 3.6 miles (5.8 km) one way with easy going at first but then some very steep sections. "Take plenty of water and oxygen" the space agency advised would-be hikers.

● The face is on the Cydonia region in the north of Mars. When Mars Global Surveyor arrived in 1998, the cloudy winter made it difficult to photograph the surface. Conspiracy theorists thought this was suspicious, but the spacecraft waited until a summer day in 2001 and recorded wonderfully clear photos.

● The first NASA space probe to fly pass Mars was *Mariner 4* in 1965. The first to orbit the Red Planet was *Mariner 9* in 1971. Finally *Viking Orbiter 1* became the first craft to land safely in 1976 and then, in May 2008, *Phoenix* successfully landed and discovered frozen water.

The most publicized event in UFO history was the crash of some unknown craft near Roswell, New Mexico, on July 7, 1947. The U.S. military said they had recovered a "flying disk" but the next day changed this to a weather balloon. More than 30 years later, in 1978, Major Jesse Marcel, who had helped recover the debris, said he believed it had been an alien spacecraft. The U.S. government held an inquiry that concluded the debris came from a top-secret spy balloon. More mysteries were hidden in Area 51, a military base in Nevada so secret the government refused to admit it existed until 1997. It is heavily guarded, and some people believe underground areas exist under the runways where UFOs and aliens were taken and examined. One rumor says the U.S. government has a pact with aliens that allows them to land at Area 51.

▶ The Roswell area has become the worldwide symbol of UFO activity and government coverups, whether true or not. This was strengthened by *The National Enquirer* running a 1980 interview with Jesse Marcel and then a claim nine years later by a former mortician that autopsies of aliens had been carried out in Roswell. Skeptics say they are unreliable witnesses. They also point out that the Roswell crash supposedly happened a year after the popular science fiction movie *Close Encounter of the Third Kind* had stirred the public's imagination about aliens. The controversy continues with both sides unable or unwilling to prove anything.

Where in the World?

The Foster Ranch is 75 miles (121 km) north of Roswell, which is the seat of Chaves County in southeastern New Mexico. Area 51 is near Groom Lake (actually a dry salt flat) in southwestern Nevada.

● AREA 51

Did You Know?

● The mysterious crash has turned Roswell into a major tourist attraction. The city holds an annual "Amazing Roswell UFO Festival," featuring an alien costume contest, parade, music, and guest speakers and authors. The town also has two UFO museums, and visitors can shop for souvenirs related to the 1947 event.

● The crash debris was found on the Foster Ranch in New Mexico. William "Max" Brazel, the ranch foreman, stumbled upon the bright debris and called the local sheriff. He said the military arrived and attempted to assemble the pieces but gave up and transported them to Roswell Army Air Field.

● The science-fiction series *Roswell* ran on American television from 1999 to 2002. The story focused on four teenage alien survivors from the famous crash. They have added human DNA to their bodies to pass as normal humans in Roswell. Love soon develops between alien Max and local girl Liz.

Alien Abduction

Betty and Barney Hill of Portsmouth, New Hampshire, were driving home late at night on September 19, 1961, when a spaceship hovered in front of their car. Barney saw humanoid figures peering out of the craft's window, and a voice commanded, "Stay where you are and keep looking." He drove away at high speed, but at home they found that their memories lacked three hours. Betty soon had nightmares of being forced with Barney toward a large, disk-shaped metallic craft by two men about 5 feet (1.5 m) tall. They had gray skin and spoke broken English. They conducted physical exams on both and used a star map to show Betty where they came from. Later, under hypnosis, she was able to draw it with details not yet known to science. The press covered their story in 1965, and it became the first UFO abduction account. Barney died in 1969 and Betty in 2004.

▶ The day after a front-page story about their abduction was run in the *Boston Traveler* on October 25, 1965, the Hills began receiving telephone calls from Europe asking for their story. They were in constant demand by the media for the rest of their lives. Sessions of hypnosis with Dr. Benjamin Simon, a Boston psychiatrist, enabled them to remember more details, such as Barney screaming "I've gotta get outta here!" when he saw the aliens. They also recalled the aliens' amazement when they discovered Barney's false teeth that came out, a fact that next had them tugging on Betty's real teeth.

Did You Know?

● The Hills were respected members of their community and at first went to great lengths to avoid any publicity. They feared that people would ridicule their story, shun them, and that they would both lose their jobs. Barney was employed by the Post Office and Betty worked for the State Welfare Agency.

● Two days after their experience, the Hills informed officers at the Pease Air Force Base. Major Paul W. Henderson visited them for a 30-minute interview. His assessment was that they had thought the planet Jupiter was a spaceship, and this report was included in the Air Force's official UFO file.

● John G. Fuller published the Hills' story in 1966 as *The Interrupted Journey*. The 1975 made-for-TV movie *The UFO Incident* was based on the book, and it starred James Earl Jones and Estelle Parsons as Barney and Betty Hills. Betty's own book, *A Common Sense Approach to UFOs*, was published in 1995.

Where in the World?

The Hills first saw the spaceship's light near Groveton in the northern part of New Hampshire, and it soon stopped them near Indian Head. Afterwards they drove to their Portsmouth home in south New Hampshire.

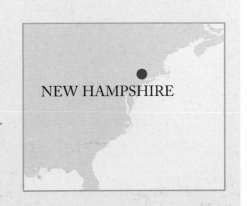

NEW HAMPSHIRE

Men in Black

Whenever a UFO appears, the Men in Black (MIB) soon arrive to hush up the event. This urban legend claims these frightening men, who usually travel in threes or alone, represent aliens or the U.S. government. Some say they are extraterrestrials themselves. The MIB wear black shiny suits and drive expensive black cars. They will use vague or direct threats to keep eyewitnesses silent or just try to convince them the event never happened. Some reports say they use strange instruments to wipe victims' memories. They will also confiscate any photos or other items connected to a sighting. The MIB seem to know everything about those they visit. They look alike, with dark complexions and slanted eyes often hidden behind sunglasses. Some MIBs act almost like robots, but others are warm and friendly.

▶ No one would want a visit from the shadowy Men in Black. Their frightening appearance is heightened by their emotionless faces and monotone voices that almost sound like computers. Conspiracy theorists point out that members of government intelligence agencies are normally required to wear dark suits. The MIB often arrive at night in a luxury car without the headlights on. The term "Men in Black" is also used today for individuals who appear near a UFO sighting and act in a strange or threatening manner. It is even applied in a wider sense to corporate officials who tend to dress alike.

Where in the World?

Men in Black will travel to any UFO site, but they have been sighted mostly in the United States in recent times. The first MIB confrontation, with Albert K. Bender, took place in Bridgeport, Connecticut.

CONNECTICUT ●

Did You Know?

• The first report of Men in Black was made in 1953 by Albert K. Bender, who published *Space Review*. He wrote that he possessed information explaining flying saucers, but three men in black suits and hats ordered him to withhold it. He complied because their threats made him "scared to death."

• The 1997 movie *Men in Black* was about a secret agency controlling alien activity on Earth. The MIB agents are played by Tommy Lee Jones and Will Smith; they must save the Galaxy from a "Bug" alien. The movie was based on the comic book series "The Men in Black."

• In his 1990 book, *Mystery of the Men in Black: The UFO Silencers*, Timothy Green Beckley claims that the MIB have been among us for hundreds of years. He links them to encounters with witches and other mysterious forms, such as the Elizabethan Black Men and the Native Americans' Black Man.

Crop Circles

Beautiful, complex designs have appeared for hundreds of years in wheat and other grain fields around the world, especially in England, in the county of Wiltshire. One formation appearing overnight there in 2001 was made up of 409 circles covering more than 12 acres (5 hectares). Arguments still rage on how the stalks were bent into such intricate patterns. In 1991, two men from Southampton, England, admitted their group, the Circlemakers, had been creating the field "art" for some 20 years using planks and tape. But many believe the most amazing designs are due to paranormal activity or may be messages from aliens in UFOs, for lights have been seen over crop circle sites. Others believe lightning, freak tornadoes, or ionized air columns may be the source. Scientists conducting experiments on the bent stalks have found that their structure was changed by some unknown energy.

▶ Hoaxers have claimed they measure out artificial crop circles with simple tools, but the more spectacular designs would seem impossible to create overnight. A two-year British study in 1999 concluded that 20 percent of the circles did not show signs of human involvement. More than 12,000 formations have been reported in the U.S., Canada, Russia, Australia, China, South Africa, and many other countries where nobody has claimed credit for this new form of art. The whole phenomenon has created two new words: "cereology" is the study of crop circles; "croppies" are people who do research on the formations.

Where in the World?

Besides England, crop circles have been discovered in numerous countries, including the USA, Canada, Australia, Japan, and Russia. The locations are often surprising, such as circles appearing in east Tennessee in 2007 and 2008.

TENNESSEE

Did You Know?

● Although some farmers complain about the circles flattening their crops, others have turned the phenomenon into a money-making venture. When a circle appeared near Wiltshire's ancient Stonehenge monument in 1996, one enterprising farmer quickly set up a small booth and charged admission, earning some £30,000 ($47,000) in four weeks.

● John Lundberg, who creates crop circles, says he sighted a UFO while making one. "It was a black cigar shape with very fast strobing lights," he said. "It appeared on the horizon and slowly arced over us, completely silent." He has also seen balls of cracking light next to fields.

● Another UFO sighting happened in 1966 in Tull, a town in Queensland, Australia. A farmer watched a flying saucer rise over his crop of sugar cane and then zoom away. When he hurried over to its lift-off site, he discovered reeds woven into an intricate pattern that was strong enough to hold ten men.

Alligators in New York Sewers

The most widely told urban myth is probably the story of alligators breeding and living in the vast sewer system of New York City. In the late 1930s, rich New Yorkers vacationing in Florida brought baby alligators home to their children. In 1935, two youths shoveling snow down a Manhattan manhole spied an alligator thrashing about below and killed it with their shovels. The beast measured 8 feet (2.4 m), and this began the rumor that families were flushing their pet gators down toilets when they became too big. The idea was strengthened that same year when workers discovered several alligators measuring about 2 feet (61 cm) each. Within two years, the city had exterminated them, using poisoned bait and flooding the tunnels they occupied. Stories persist that the large descendants remain and some have become albino white and blind, though none of these have been seen.

▶ It would be hard work to flush a wiggling alligator down the toilet, especially if it had grown too large to keep. The city's commissioner of sewers, Teddy May, believed the ones in the sewer had been forced down storm drains. It was much easier in ancient times for alligators and crocodiles to live in nearby urban sewers, many of which were open. Crocodiles, for example, are thought to have been in the sewer system of medieval Constantinople. This type of story is an old one still alive in modern folklore, according to the urban myth expert Jan Harold Brunvand.

Where in the World?

The New York City sewer system, consisting of 6,600 miles (10,629 km) of pipes, runs under the five boroughs of the Bronx, Brooklyn, Manhattan, Queens, and Staten Island. The first alligator was caught under East 123rd Street.

NEW YORK

Did You Know?

● Experts say alligators could not thrive under New York City or reproduce in that environment. The area would be freezing during the winter, and alligators always need warmth to survive. If they never surfaced, they could survive eating rats and trash, but the polluted sewer water would soon kill them.

● When sewer works reported alligators in 1935 to their commissioner, he had teams investigate the sewer. This ended when he made his own inspection and saw alligators in the beam of his flashlight.

● City officials do not believe people flush alligators down their toilets because they would not fit through. They suspect that the first 1935 alligator probably arrived on a steamer. The only recent encounters in 2001 and 2006 were of caimans (small crocodiles) that were probably pets let loose on the street.

The Mexican Pet

Many versions exist about the kind woman who adopts an ugly dog. The original, dating back to the early 1980s, tells of a couple from La Mesa, California, who visit a Mexican town and find this small, loving, but ugly, dog. The woman feeds it during their vacation and lets it cuddle up in bed with them. Knowing the rules against bringing a dog into the United States, she smuggles him successfully across the border. Arriving home, she bathes the poor creature and settles it into their bed as it licks her face. The next morning, the animal is foaming at the mouth. She rushes him to the veterinarian who asks sharply, "Where did you get this dog?" She lies that it was a neighborhood stray. The vet shakes his head and says, "You didn't find it here. This is not a dog. It's a Mexican sewer rat, and it's dying."

▶ Smuggling a Mexican animal into the United States is not easy, but stories of success are becoming more frequent. The source of the pet is often Tijuana, where, as one tale says, a woman returning home notices that her new "chihuahua's" eyes are runny and is soon informed of the terrible truth. In another version, the pet chews through the kitchen wall into the garage. "The Mexican Pet" is such a widely told story that it was used as the title of a book of local legends by Jan Harold Brunvand, a professor of English at the University of Utah.

Where in the World?

The family in the original story is from La Mesa, California, in San Diego County on the Mexican border. They visit Tijuana, Mexico, just over the border. Other U.S. versions are set in Texas towns.

● SAN DIEGO COUNTY

Did You Know?

● Some versions do not mention Mexico. The dog turns out to be a rat from Korea, China, Hong Kong, Haiti, and so on. A Florida story has men rescuing a pathetic dog from the sea and bringing it home where it eats the pet cat and turns out to be a Guatemalan rat.

● The Mexican Pet story began as the Turkish Pet. It is a myth in many countries and always involves the rat dying or killing the family's real pet.

● An unusual telling is about a family who tied their puppy to their car at the beach. They returned to find it stolen but luckily saw a mangy dog needing love. Their vet quickly informed them it was a dock rat, and they then realized this rat had eaten their puppy.

Giant Man-eating Catfish

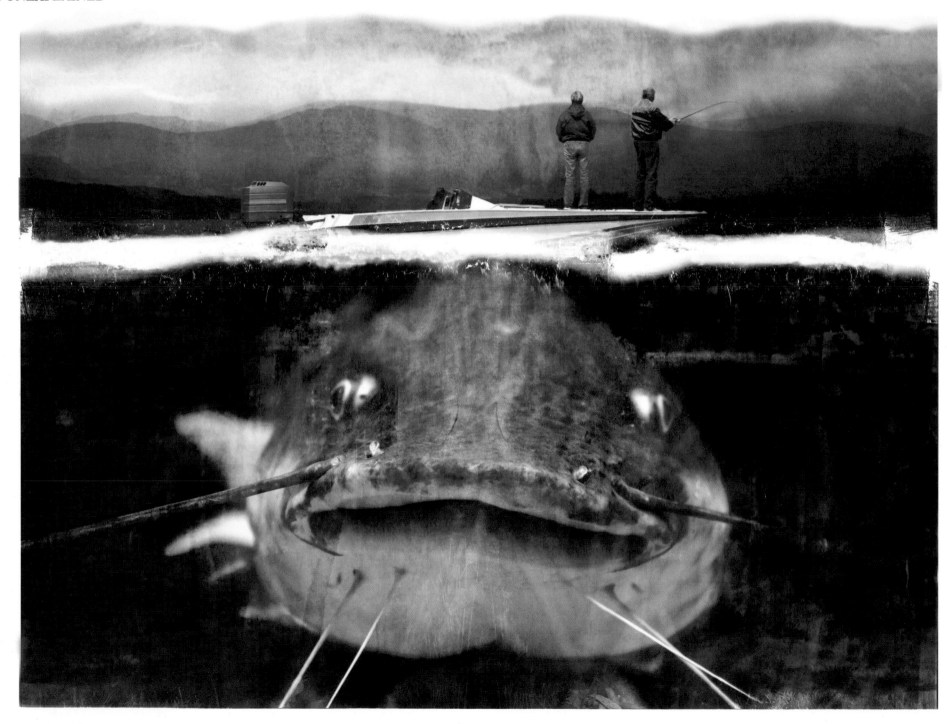

Fishermen have long told tales of giant man-eating catfish. In American states, a persistent local legend from the 1950s is about scuba divers inspecting a dam when they spot a catfish "as large as a Volkswagen." The terrified divers refuse to stay in the water for fear the beast would swallow them whole. It is true that catfish are voracious and aggressive predators, and giant ones are considered to be extremely dangerous. An 8-foot (2.4-m) Mekong catfish weighing 646 pounds (292 kg) was caught recently in Thailand, and wels catfish in Europe can grow to be several hundred pounds. Fish biologists say a very large catfish might try to swallow a human, but it would not be successful. They are scavengers that usually feed on plants, but some have developed a taste for animals. In 2004, one giant specimen in a German lake is believed to have pulled a dachshund underwater and eaten him.

▶ The American myth of catfish terrifying scuba divers near dams is more than 50 years old, and stories persist across the country and on the Internet. Fishery biologists in Alabama alone report hearing the story dozens of times a year. Unlike the larger species found in Asia and Europe, a monstrous catfish in the United States might weigh close to 200 pounds (90 kg). Biologists say a catfish of this size would not come close to eating even a small child. This does not stop an American story of car-sized catfish seen by dam maintenance divers whose hair turned white from the shock.

Where in the World?

Giant catfish are found around the world. The very large Wallago attu lives in Thailand, Java, India, and Burma. The equally impressive wels catfish exists throughout Europe, and the endangered Mekong giant catfish is found in Asia.

THAILAND

Did You Know?

• Controversy surrounded photos taken of a 10-foot (3-m) "man-eating catfish" caught in 2007 in China's Furong Reservoir in Huadu. Locals say they cut it open and discovered the remains of a man inside. The local government supposedly banned news of the catch, and swimming in the reservoir is now forbidden.

• In his book *Life on the Mississippi*, published in 1883, Mark Twain, who was himself a fisherman, relates the story of a 250-pound (112.5-kg) catfish. Twain also once said, "Do not tell fish stories where people know you; but particularly don't tell them where people know the fish."

• Greedy catfish can get into trouble. One died in 2008 in Germany's Main River when it tried to eat a soccerball. In 2004 in Wichita, Kansas, one got a child's basketball stuck in its throat. The buoyancy of the ball kept the fish on the surface. However, someone punctured the ball and the fish swam away unharmed.

Bridey Murphy

Is it possible that we have led past lives? The theory of reincarnation received a boost in 1956 when Virginia Tighe, a 33-year-old housewife in Pueblo, Colorado, gave detailed accounts of her previous life in nineteenth-century Ireland. The story of her existence as Bridey Murphy, who supposedly lived from 1798 to 1864, was told during six sessions of hypnosis. She even spoke in an Irish brogue as she recalled streets and neighbors in her former city of Cork. To check out these details, the *Denver Post*, which had broken the story, sent a reporter to Cork. He found some of the places and said her descriptions were accurate, but there were no records of a Bridey Murphy. Of the people she recalled, only the grocer's name was found. Worse, a Chicago newspaper reported that Tighe had lived across the street from a Bridey Murphy Corkell as a child.

▶ Morey Bernstein, a Pueblo amateur hypnotist, was surprised when Virginia Tighe recounted her former life in a trance. He recorded the hypnotic sessions and wrote *The Search for Bridey Murphy*. Some newspapers accused Tighe and Bernstein of fraud. "Well, it's no fraud, whatever it is," said William Barker, the reporter who wrote the *Denver Post* story and checked it out in Ireland. "All I think we've proved definitely is that memory is unreliable. And that we know less than nothing about our brains and our souls." Americans seemed to agree, as open-minded debates on reincarnation took place around the country.

Where in the World?

Virginia Tighe's hometown of Pueblo, Colorado, is in the southern part of the state 103 miles (166 km) south of Denver. Bridey grew up in Cork, Ireland, which is a major seaport on the eastern coast.

● COLORADO

Did You Know?

● The 1956 book, *The Search for Bridey Murphy*, sold millions of copies in more than 30 languages and was made into a movie that year. Thousands of records were sold of Tighe speaking as Bridey in her first session of hypnosis. Several popular songs about Bridey were also recorded.

● The Bridey Murphy phenomenon began a nationwide craze for reincarnation in the United States. Hypnotists began offering sessions to find your prior existence, with one charging $25 an existence. Many Americans suddenly decided they must have lived before, some as English princesses, French peasants, and even one as a horse.

● Bridey said she was born on December 20, 1798, the red-headed daughter of a lawyer, Duncan Murphy, and his wife, Kathleen. She married a lawyer named Sean McCarthy when she was 17 and they moved to Belfast. Bridey said she had died after a bad fall and remembered watching her own funeral.

Index